God's Promises®
for
Mothers

God's Promises®
for
Mothers

Published by
Thomas Nelson
Since 1798
www.thomasnelson.com

Published in Nashville, Tennessee, by Thomas Nelson, Inc.

Thomas Nelson, Inc. titles may be purchased in bulk for educational, business, fund-raising, or sales promotional use. For information, please e-mail SpecialMarkets@ThomasNelson.com.

Compiled by Kay Kilgore Wheeler.
Cover design by Greg Jackson, ThinkPen Design.

ISBN-10: 1-4041-1327-4 (NKJV)
ISBN-13: 978-1-4041-1327-5 (NKJV)
ISBN-10: 1-4041-1342-8 (SS)
ISBN-13: 978-1-4041-1342-8 (SS)

Printed in the United States of America
07 08 09 10 11 BANTA 9 8 7 6 5 4 3 2 1

Contents

Mothers of the Bible

Mothers' Prayers in the Bible

The Responsibilities of Motherhood

The Promises of Motherhood

The Blessings of Motherhood

God's Answers for Mothers

Scripture Meditations for Mothers

Crisis Scripture Guide for Mothers

Introduction

Perhaps there is no greater privilege in life than having a godly mother, one who fears the Lord and stands in the gap in prayer for her children. How many of us can trace our first witness of truth and salvation to our own precious mothers? How many of us experienced true understanding and the unconditional love of Jesus through a motherly example? Even God Himself used the analogy of a mother's love to express His love for His people: "But Zion said, 'The LORD has forsaken me, and my Lord has forgotten me.' Can a woman forget her nursing child, and not have compassion on the son of her womb? . . . See, I have inscribed you on the palms of My hands; your walls are continually before Me." (Isaiah 49:14–16) There are many blessings, promises, responsibilities, and examples of motherhood in the Bible. A woman who abides in Christ and walks in His ways may cherish and claim this rich inheritance God has provided. This volume of God's Holy Word is dedicated to all mothers for encouragement, assurance, comfort, and hope; so shall it be that "her children rise up and call her blessed; her husband also, and he praises her" (Proverbs 31:28).

Mothers of
the Bible

Abigail
(Wife of David)

Now when Abigail saw David, she dismounted quickly from the donkey, fell on her face before David, and bowed down to the ground.

So she fell at his feet and said: "On me, my lord, on me let this iniquity be! And please let your maidservant speak in your ears, and hear the words of your maidservant."

I Samuel 25:23–24

When the servants of David had come to Abigail at Carmel, they spoke to her saying, "David sent us to you, to ask you to become his wife."

Then she arose, bowed her face to the earth, and said, "Here is your maidservant, a servant to wash the feet of the servants of my lord."

So Abigail rose in haste and rode on a donkey, attended by five of her maidens; and she followed the messengers of David, and became his wife.

I Samuel 25:40–42

His second, Chileab, by Abigail the widow of Nabal the Carmelite; the third, Absalom the son of Maacah, the daughter of Talmai, king of Geshur;

the fourth, Adonijah the son of Haggith; the fifth, Shephatiah the son of Abital;

and the sixth, Ithream, by David's wife Eglah. These were born to David in Hebron.

II Samuel 3:3–5

Bathsheba

(Mother of Solomon)

Then she said to him, "My lord, you swore by the LORD your God to your maidservant, saying, 'Assuredly Solomon your son shall reign after me, and he shall sit on my throne.'"

I Kings 1:17

Then King David answered and said, "Call Bathsheba to me." So she came into the king's presence and stood before the king.

And the king took an oath and said, "As the LORD lives, who has redeemed my life from every distress,

"just as I swore to you by the LORD God of Israel, saying, 'Assuredly Solomon your son shall be king after me, and he shall sit on my throne in my place,' so I certainly will do this day."

I Kings 1:28–30

Then Bathsheba bowed with her face to the earth, and paid homage to the king, and said, "Let my lord King David live forever!"

I Kings 1:31

Go forth, O daughters of Zion,
And see King Solomon with the crown
With which his mother crowned him
On the day of his wedding,
The day of the gladness of his heart.

Song of Solomon 3:11

Elect Lady
(II John)

The Elder,
To the elect lady and her children, whom I love in truth, and not only I, but also all those who have known the truth.

II John 1

I rejoiced greatly that I have found some of your children walking in truth, as we received commandment from the Father.

And now I plead with you, lady, not as though I wrote a new commandment to you, but that which we have had from the beginning: that we love one another.

II John 4–5

Elizabeth
❧
(Mother of John the Baptist)

There was in the days of Herod, the king of Judea, a certain priest named Zacharias, of the division of Abijah. His wife was of the daughters of Aaron, and her name was Elizabeth.

And they were both righteous before God, walking in all the commandments and ordinances of the Lord blameless.

But they had no child, because Elizabeth was barren, and they were both well advanced in years.

Luke 1:5–7

But the angel said to him, "Do not be afraid, Zacharias, for your prayer is heard; and your wife Elizabeth will bear you a son, and you shall call his name John."

Luke 1:13

Now after those days his wife Elizabeth conceived; and she hid herself five months, saying,

"Thus the Lord has dealt with me, in the days when He looked on me, to take away my reproach among people."

Luke 1:24–25

"Now indeed, Elizabeth your relative has also conceived a son in her old age; and this is now the sixth month for her who was called barren.

"For with God nothing will be impossible."

Luke 1:36–37

And it happened, when Elizabeth heard the greeting of Mary, that the babe leaped in her womb; and Elizabeth was filled with the Holy Spirit.

Then she spoke out with a loud voice and said, "Blessed are you among women, and blessed is the fruit of your womb!

"But why is this granted to me, that the mother of my Lord should come to me?

"For indeed, as soon as the voice of your greeting sounded in my ears, the babe leaped in my womb for joy.

"Blessed is she who believed, for there will be a fulfillment of those things which were told her from the Lord."

Luke 1:41–45

Now Elizabeth's full time came for her to be delivered, and she brought forth a son.

When her neighbors and relatives heard how the Lord had shown great mercy to her, they rejoiced with her.

Luke 1:57–58

"And you, child, will be called the prophet of the Highest;
For you will go before the face of the Lord to prepare His ways,
To give knowledge of salvation to His people
By the remission of their sins."

Luke 1:76–77

Eunice
(Mother of Timothy)

This is a faithful saying and worthy of all acceptance, that Christ Jesus came into the world to save sinners, of whom I am chief.

I Timothy 1:15

Then he came to Derbe and Lystra. And behold, a certain disciple was there, named Timothy, the son of a certain Jewish woman who believed, but his father was Greek.

Acts 16:1

Eve
❧
(Mother of All Living)

"And I will put enmity
Between you and the woman,
And between your seed and her Seed;
He shall bruise your head,
And you shall bruise His heel."

Genesis 3:15

And Adam called his wife's name Eve, because she was the mother of all living.

Genesis 3:20

Now Adam knew Eve his wife, and she conceived and bore Cain, and said, "I have acquired a man from the LORD."

Then she bore again, this time his brother Abel. Now Abel was a keeper of sheep, but Cain was a tiller of the ground.

Genesis 4:1–2

And Adam knew his wife again, and she bore a son and named him Seth, "For God has appointed another seed for me instead of Abel, whom Cain killed."

Genesis 4:25

Hagar

❧ (Mother of Ishmael)

Now the Angel of the LORD found her by a spring of water in the wilderness, by the spring on the way to Shur.

And He said, "Hagar, Sarai's maid, where have you come from, and where are you going?" She said, "I am fleeing from the presence of my mistress Sarai."

The Angel of the LORD said to her, "Return to your mistress, and submit yourself under her hand."

Then the Angel of the LORD said to her, "I will multiply your descendants exceedingly, so that they shall not be counted for multitude."

And the Angel of the LORD said to her:
"Behold, you are with child,
And you shall bear a son.
You shall call his name Ishmael,
Because the LORD has heard your affliction."

Genesis 16:7–11

Then she went and sat down across from him at a distance of about a bowshot; for she said to herself, "Let me not see the death of the boy." So she sat opposite him, and lifted her voice and wept.

And God heard the voice of the lad. Then the angel of God called to Hagar out of heaven, and said to her, "What ails you, Hagar? Fear not, for God has heard the voice of the lad where he is.

"Arise, lift up the lad and hold him with your hand, for I will make him a great nation."

Then God opened her eyes, and she saw a well of water. And she went and filled the skin with water, and gave the lad a drink.

Genesis 21:16–19

Hannah

(Mother of Samuel)

And she was in bitterness of soul, and prayed to the LORD and wept in anguish.

Then she made a vow and said, "O LORD of hosts, if You will indeed look on the affliction of Your maidservant and remember me, and not forget Your maidservant, but will give Your maidservant a male child, then I will give him to the LORD all the days of his life, and no razor shall come upon his head."

I Samuel 1:10–11

So it came to pass in the process of time that Hannah conceived and bore a son, and called his name Samuel, saying, "Because I have asked for him from the LORD."

I Samuel 1:20

"For this child I prayed, and the LORD has granted me my petition which I asked of Him.

"Therefore I also have lent him to the LORD; as long as he lives he shall be lent to the LORD." So they worshiped the LORD there.

I Samuel 1:27–28

And Hannah prayed and said:
"My heart rejoices in the LORD;
My horn is exalted in the LORD.
I smile at my enemies,
Because I rejoice in Your salvation.
No one is holy like the LORD,
For there is none besides You,
Nor is there any rock like our God.
Talk no more so very proudly;
Let no arrogance come from your mouth,
For the LORD is the God of knowledge;
And by Him actions are weighed.
The bows of the mighty men are broken,
And those who stumbled are girded with strength.
Those who were full have hired themselves out
for bread,
And the hungry have ceased to hunger.
Even the barren has borne seven,
And she who has many children has become feeble.
The LORD kills and makes alive;
He brings down to the grave and brings up.
The LORD makes poor and makes rich;
He brings low and lifts up.
He raises the poor from the dust
And lifts the beggar from the ash heap,
To set them among princes
And make them inherit the throne of glory.

For the pillars of the earth are the LORD's,
And He has set the world upon them.
He will guard the feet of His saints,
But the wicked shall be silent in darkness.
For by strength no man shall prevail.
The adversaries of the LORD shall be broken
in pieces;
From heaven He will thunder against them.
The LORD will judge the ends of the earth.
He will give strength to His king,
And exalt the horn of His anointed."

I Samuel 2:1–10

And the LORD visited Hannah, so that she conceived and bore three sons and two daughters. Meanwhile the child Samuel grew before the LORD.

I Samuel 2:21

Jedidah
❧
(Mother of King Josiah)

Josiah was eight years old when he became king, and he reigned thirty-one years in Jerusalem. His mother's name was Jedidah the daughter of Adaiah of Bozkath.

And he did what was right in the sight of the LORD, and walked in all the ways of his father David; he did not turn aside to the right hand or to the left.

II Kings 22:1–2

Now before him there was no king like him, who turned to the LORD with all his heart, with all his soul, and with all his might, according to all the Law of Moses; nor after him did any arise like him.

II Kings 23:25

Jochebed

(Mother of Moses, Aaron, and Miriam)

And a man of the house of Levi went and took as wife a daughter of Levi.

So the woman conceived and bore a son. And when she saw that he was a beautiful child, she hid him three months.

But when she could no longer hide him, she took an ark of bulrushes for him, daubed it with asphalt and pitch, put the child in it, and laid it in the reeds by the river's bank.

And his sister stood afar off, to know what would be done to him.

Exodus 2:1–4

Now Amram took for himself Jochebed, his father's sister, as wife; and she bore him Aaron and Moses. And the years of the life of Amram were one hundred and thirty-seven.

Exodus 6:20

The name of Amram's wife was Jochebed the daughter of Levi, who was born to Levi in Egypt; and to Amram she bore Aaron and Moses and their sister Miriam.

Numbers 26:59

Leah

❧

(Mother of Reuben, Simeon, Levi, Judah, Issachar, Zebulun, and Dinah)

When the LORD saw that Leah was unloved, He opened her womb; but Rachel was barren.

So Leah conceived and bore a son, and she called his name Reuben; for she said, "The LORD has surely looked on my affliction. Now therefore, my husband will love me."

Then she conceived again and bore a son, and said, "Because the LORD has heard that I am unloved, He has therefore given me this son also." And she called his name Simeon.

She conceived again and bore a son, and said, "Now this time my husband will become attached to me, because I have borne him three sons." Therefore his name was called Levi.

And she conceived again and bore a son, and said, "Now I will praise the LORD." Therefore she called his name Judah. Then she stopped bearing.

Genesis 29:31–35

Then Leah conceived again and bore Jacob a sixth son.

And Leah said, "God has endowed me with a good endowment; now my husband will dwell with me, because I have borne him six sons." So she called his name Zebulun.

Afterward she bore a daughter, and called her name Dinah.

Genesis 30:19–21

Mary
(Mother of Jesus)

Now in the sixth month the angel Gabriel was sent by God to a city of Galilee named Nazareth,

to a virgin betrothed to a man whose name was Joseph, of the house of David. The virgin's name was Mary.

And having come in, the angel said to her, "Rejoice, highly favored one, the Lord is with you; blessed are you among women!"

But when she saw him, she was troubled at his saying, and considered what manner of greeting this was.

Then the angel said to her, "Do not be afraid, Mary, for you have found favor with God.

"And behold, you will conceive in your womb and bring forth a Son, and shall call His name JESUS."

Luke 1:26–31

Then she spoke out with a loud voice and said, "Blessed are you among women, and blessed is the fruit of your womb!"

Luke 1:42

And Mary said:
"My soul magnifies the Lord,

And my spirit has rejoiced in God my Savior.
For He has regarded the lowly state of His
maidservant;
For behold, henceforth all generations will call
me blessed.
For He who is mighty has done great things for me,
And holy is His name.
And His mercy is on those who fear Him
From generation to generation.
He has shown strength with His arm;
He has scattered the proud in the imagination of
their hearts.
He has put down the mighty from their thrones,
And exalted the lowly.
He has filled the hungry with good things,
And the rich He has sent away empty.

Luke 1:46–53

Now there stood by the cross of Jesus His mother, and His mother's sister, Mary the wife of Clopas, and Mary Magdalene.

When Jesus therefore saw His mother, and the disciple whom He loved standing by, He said to His mother, "Woman, behold your son!"

Then He said to the disciple, "Behold your mother!" And from that hour that disciple took her to his own home.

John 19:25–27

On the third day there was a wedding in Cana of Galilee, and the mother of Jesus was there.

Now both Jesus and His disciples were invited to the wedding.

And when they ran out of wine, the mother of Jesus said to Him, "They have no wine."

Jesus said to her, "Woman, what does your concern have to do with Me? My hour has not yet come."

His mother said to the servants, "Whatever He says to you, do it."

John 2:1–5

Midwives to the Hebrews
❧
(Shiphrah and Puah)

Then the king of Egypt spoke to the Hebrew midwives, of whom the name of one was Shiphrah and the name of the other Puah;

and he said, "When you do the duties of a midwife for the Hebrew women, and see them on the birthstools, if it is a son, then you shall kill him; but if it is a daughter, then she shall live."

But the midwives feared God, and did not do as the king of Egypt commanded them, but saved the male children alive.

So the king of Egypt called for the midwives and said to them, "Why have you done this thing, and saved the male children alive?"

And the midwives said to Pharaoh, "Because the Hebrew women are not like the Egyptian women; for they are lively and give birth before the midwives come to them."

Therefore God dealt well with the midwives, and the people multiplied and grew very mighty.

And so it was, because the midwives feared God, that He provided households for them.

So Pharaoh commanded all his people, saying, "Every son who is born you shall cast into the river, and every daughter you shall save alive."

Exodus 1:15–22

Mother
❈
(Of Blind Son)

Now as Jesus passed by, He saw a man who was blind from birth.

And His disciples asked Him, saying, "Rabbi, who sinned, this man or his parents, that he was born blind?"

Jesus answered, "Neither this man nor his parents sinned, but that the works of God should be revealed in him."

John 9:1–3

And they asked them, saying, "Is this your son, who you say was born blind? How then does he now see?"

His parents answered them and said, "We know that this is our son, and that he was born blind."

John 9:19–20

Mother

❧

(Proverbs 31)

Who can find a virtuous wife?
For her worth is far above rubies.
The heart of her husband safely trusts her;
So he will have no lack of gain.
She does him good and not evil
All the days of her life.
She seeks wool and flax,
And willingly works with her hands.
She is like the merchant ships,
She brings her food from afar.
She also rises while it is yet night,
And provides food for her household,
And a portion for her maidservants.

Proverbs 31:10–15

Strength and honor are her clothing;
She shall rejoice in time to come.
She opens her mouth with wisdom,
And on her tongue is the law of kindness.
She watches over the ways of her household,
And does not eat the bread of idleness.
Her children rise up and call her blessed;

Her husband also, and he praises her:
"Many daughters have done well,
But you excel them all."
Charm is deceitful and beauty is passing,
But a woman who fears the LORD, she shall
be praised.
Give her of the fruit of her hands,
And let her own works praise her in the gates.

Proverbs 31:25–31

Mother
❧
(In Solomon's Time)

And the king said, "Divide the living child in two, and give half to one, and half to the other."

Then the woman whose son was living spoke to the king, for she yearned with compassion for her son; and she said, "O my lord, give her the living child, and by no means kill him!" But the other said, "Let him be neither mine nor yours, but divide him."

So the king answered and said, "Give the first woman the living child, and by no means kill him; she is his mother."

And all Israel heard of the judgment which the king had rendered; and they feared the king, for they saw that the wisdom of God was in him to administer justice.

I Kings 3:25–28

Mother
❦
(Of Zebedee's Children)

Among whom were Mary Magdalene, Mary the mother of James and Joses, and the mother of Zebedee's sons.

Matthew 27:56

Then the mother of Zebedee's sons came to Him with her sons, kneeling down and asking something from Him.

And He said to her, "What do you wish?" She said to Him, "Grant that these two sons of mine may sit, one on Your right hand and the other on the left, in Your kingdom."

Matthew 20:20–21

Nain Widow
(Mother of One Son)

Now it happened, the day after, that He went into a city called Nain; and many of His disciples went with Him, and a large crowd.

And when He came near the gate of the city, behold, a dead man was being carried out, the only son of his mother; and she was a widow. And a large crowd from the city was with her.

When the Lord saw her, He had compassion on her and said to her, "Do not weep."

Then He came and touched the open coffin, and those who carried him stood still. And He said, "Young man, I say to you, arise."

So he who was dead sat up and began to speak. And He presented him to his mother.

Then fear came upon all, and they glorified God, saying, "A great prophet has risen up among us"; and, "God has visited His people."

And this report about Him went throughout all Judea and all the surrounding region.

Then the disciples of John reported to him concerning all these things.

And John, calling two of his disciples to him, sent them to Jesus, saying, "Are You the Coming One, or do we look for another?"

Luke 7:11–19

Naomi
(Ruth's Mother-in-Law)

And Naomi said to her two daughters-in-law, "Go, return each to her mother's house. The LORD deal kindly with you, as you have dealt with the dead and with me.

"The LORD grant that you may find rest, each in the house of her husband." So she kissed them, and they lifted up their voices and wept.

Ruth 1:8–9

But Ruth said:
"Entreat me not to leave you,
Or to turn back from following after you;
For wherever you go, I will go;
And wherever you lodge, I will lodge;
Your people shall be my people,
And your God, my God."

Ruth 1:16

Then they lifted up their voices and wept again; and Orpah kissed her mother-in-law, but Ruth clung to her.

"Where you die, I will die,

And there will I be buried.
The LORD do so to me, and more also,
If anything but death parts you and me."

Ruth 1:14, 17

Pharaoh's Daughter
(Mothered Moses)

Then the daughter of Pharaoh came down to wash herself at the river. And her maidens walked along the riverside; and when she saw the ark among the reeds, she sent her maid to get it.

And when she opened it, she saw the child, and behold, the baby wept. So she had compassion on him, and said, "This is one of the Hebrews' children."

Then his sister said to Pharaoh's daughter, "Shall I go and call a nurse for you from the Hebrew women, that she may nurse the child for you?"

And Pharaoh's daughter said to her, "Go." So the maiden went and called the child's mother.

Then Pharaoh's daughter said to her, "Take this child away and nurse him for me, and I will give you your wages." So the woman took the child and nursed him.

And the child grew, and she brought him to Pharaoh's daughter, and he became her son. So she called his name Moses, saying, "Because I drew him out of the water."

Exodus 2:5–10

Rachel
(Mother of Joseph and Benjamin)

Now when Rachel saw that she bore Jacob no children, Rachel envied her sister, and said to Jacob, "Give me children, or else I die!"

Genesis 30:1

Then God remembered Rachel, and God listened to her and opened her womb.

And she conceived and bore a son, and said, "God has taken away my reproach."

So she called his name Joseph, and said, "The LORD shall add to me another son."

Genesis 30:22–24

Rebekah
(Mother of Jacob and Esau)

Then they called Rebekah and said to her, "Will you go with this man?" And she said, "I will go."

So they sent away Rebekah their sister and her nurse, and Abraham's servant and his men.

And they blessed Rebekah and said to her:
"Our sister, may you become
The mother of thousands of ten thousands;
And may your descendants possess
The gates of those who hate them."

Genesis 24:58–60

Ruth
❧
(Mother of Obed)

"Moreover, Ruth the Moabitess, the widow of Mahlon, I have acquired as my wife, to perpetuate the name of the dead through his inheritance, that the name of the dead may not be cut off from among his brethren and from his position at the gate. You are witnesses this day."

Ruth 4:10

So Boaz took Ruth and she became his wife; and when he went in to her, the LORD gave her conception, and she bore a son.

Ruth 4:13

Also the neighbor women gave him a name, saying, "There is a son born to Naomi." And they called his name Obed. He is the father of Jesse, the father of David.

Ruth 4:17

Obed begot Jesse, and Jesse begot David.

Ruth 4:22

Samson's Mother

❧

Then Manoah prayed to the LORD, and said, "O my Lord, please let the Man of God whom You sent come to us again and teach us what we shall do for the child who will be born."

Judges 13:8

So the Angel of the LORD said to Manoah, "Of all that I said to the woman let her be careful.

"She may not eat anything that comes from the vine, nor may she drink wine or similar drink, nor eat anything unclean. All that I commanded her let her observe."

Then Manoah said to the Angel of the LORD, "Please let us detain You, and we will prepare a young goat for You."

Judges 13:13–15

So the woman bore a son and called his name Samson; and the child grew, and the LORD blessed him.

Judges 13:24

Sarah
(Mother of Isaac)

Then God said to Abraham, "As for Sarai your wife, you shall not call her name Sarai, but Sarah shall be her name.

"And I will bless her and also give you a son by her; then I will bless her, and she shall be a mother of nations; kings of peoples shall be from her."

Genesis 17:15–16

Then God said: "No, Sarah your wife shall bear you a son, and you shall call his name Isaac; I will establish My covenant with him for an everlasting covenant, and with his descendants after him."

Genesis 17:19

And the LORD visited Sarah as He had said, and the LORD did for Sarah as He had spoken.

For Sarah conceived and bore Abraham a son in his old age, at the set time of which God had spoken to him.

And Abraham called the name of his son who was born to him—whom Sarah bore to him—Isaac.

Genesis 21:1–3

Shunammite Mother

Now it happened one day that Elisha went to Shunem, where there was a notable woman, and she persuaded him to eat some food. So it was, as often as he passed by, he would turn in there to eat some food.

And she said to her husband, "Look now, I know that this is a holy man of God, who passes by us regularly.

"Please, let us make a small upper room on the wall; and let us put a bed for him there, and a table and a chair and a lampstand; so it will be, whenever he comes to us, he can turn in there."

And it happened one day that he came there, and he turned in to the upper room and lay down there.

Then he said to Gehazi his servant, "Call this Shunammite woman." When he had called her, she stood before him.

And he said to him, "Say now to her, 'Look, you have been concerned for us with all this care. What can I do for you? Do you want me to speak on your behalf to the king or to the commander of the army?'" She answered, "I dwell among my own people."

So he said, "What then is to be done for her?" And Gehazi answered, "Actually, she has no son, and her husband is old."

So he said, "Call her." When he had called her, she stood in the doorway.

Then he said, "About this time next year you shall embrace a son." And she said, "No, my lord. Man of God, do not lie to your maidservant!"

But the woman conceived, and bore a son when the appointed time had come, of which Elisha had told her.

II Kings 4:8–17

And the child grew. Now it happened one day that he went out to his father, to the reapers.

And he said to his father, "My head, my head!" So he said to a servant, "Carry him to his mother."

When he had taken him and brought him to his mother, he sat on her knees till noon, and then died.

And she went up and laid him on the bed of the man of God, shut the door upon him, and went out.

II Kings 4:18–21

And the mother of the child said, "As the LORD lives, and as your soul lives, I will not leave you." So he arose and followed her.

Now Gehazi went on ahead of them, and laid the staff on the face of the child; but there was neither voice nor hearing. Therefore he went back to meet him, and told him, saying, "The child has not awakened."

When Elisha came into the house, there was the child, lying dead on his bed.

II Kings 4:30–32

And he called Gehazi and said, "Call this Shunammite woman." So he called her. And when she came in to him, he said, "Pick up your son."

II Kings 4:36

Syrophoenician Mother

❧

And behold, a woman of Canaan came from that region and cried out to Him, saying, "Have mercy on me, O Lord, Son of David! My daughter is severely demon-possessed."

But He answered her not a word. And His disciples came and urged Him, saying, "Send her away, for she cries out after us."

But He answered and said, "I was not sent except to the lost sheep of the house of Israel."

Then she came and worshiped Him, saying, "Lord, help me!"

But He answered and said, "It is not good to take the children's bread and throw it to the little dogs."

And she said, "Yes, Lord, yet even the little dogs eat the crumbs which fall from their masters' table."

Then Jesus answered and said to her, "O woman, great is your faith! Let it be to you as you desire." And her daughter was healed from that very hour.

Matthew 15:22–28

Widow

(With Two Sons)

A certain woman of the wives of the sons of the prophets cried out to Elisha, saying, "Your servant my husband is dead, and you know that your servant feared the LORD. And the creditor is coming to take my two sons to be his slaves."

So Elisha said to her, "What shall I do for you? Tell me, what do you have in the house?" And she said, "Your maidservant has nothing in the house but a jar of oil."

Then he said, "Go, borrow vessels from everywhere, from all your neighbors—empty vessels; do not gather just a few.

"And when you have come in, you shall shut the door behind you and your sons; then pour it into all those vessels, and set aside the full ones."

So she went from him and shut the door behind her and her sons, who brought the vessels to her; and she poured it out.

Now it came to pass, when the vessels were full, that she said to her son, "Bring me another vessel." And he said to her, "There is not another vessel." So the oil ceased.

Then she came and told the man of God. And he said, "Go, sell the oil and pay your debt; and you and your sons live on the rest."

II Kings 4:1–7

Zarephath Widow

"Arise, go to Zarephath, which belongs to Sidon, and dwell there. See, I have commanded a widow there to provide for you."

I Kings 17:9

And he stretched himself out on the child three times, and cried out to the LORD and said, "O LORD my God, I pray, let this child's soul come back to him."

Then the LORD heard the voice of Elijah; and the soul of the child came back to him, and he revived.

And Elijah took the child and brought him down from the upper room into the house, and gave him to his mother. And Elijah said, "See, your son lives!"

Then the woman said to Elijah, "Now by this I know that you are a man of God, and that the word of the LORD in your mouth is the truth."

I Kings 17:21–24

And Elijah said to her, "Do not fear; go and do as you have said, but make me a small cake from it first, and bring it to me; and afterward make some for yourself and your son.

"For thus says the LORD God of Israel: 'The bin of

flour shall not be used up, nor shall the jar of oil run dry, until the day the LORD sends rain on the earth.'"

So she went away and did according to the word of Elijah; and she and he and her household ate for many days.

I Kings 17:13–15

Zipporah
(Wife of Moses)

Then Moses was content to live with the man, and he gave Zipporah his daughter to Moses.

And she bore him a son. He called his name Gershom, for he said, "I have been a stranger in a foreign land."

Exodus 2:21–22

Then Zipporah took a sharp stone and cut off the foreskin of her son and cast it at Moses' feet, and said, "Surely you are a husband of blood to me!"

Exodus 4:25

Then Jethro, Moses' father-in-law, took Zipporah, Moses' wife, after he had sent her back,

with her two sons, of whom the name of one was Gershom (for he said, "I have been a stranger in a foreign land").

Exodus 18:2–3

Mothers' Prayers
in the Bible

Bathsheba

(Prayer for Her Child's Success and Rightful Place)

Then she said to him, "My lord, you swore by the LORD your God to your maidservant, saying, 'Assuredly Solomon your son shall reign after me, and he shall sit on my throne.'"

I Kings 1:17

Then King David answered and said, "Call Bathsheba to me." So she came into the king's presence and stood before the king.

And the king took an oath and said, "As the LORD lives, who has redeemed my life from every distress,

"just as I swore to you by the LORD God of Israel, saying, 'Assuredly Solomon your son shall be king after me, and he shall sit on my throne in my place,' so I certainly will do this day."

Then Bathsheba bowed with her face to the earth, and paid homage to the king, and said, "Let my lord King David live forever!"

I Kings 1:28–31

Deborah

(Prayer of Praise)

Then Deborah and Barak the son of Abinoam sang
on that day, saying:
"When leaders lead in Israel,
When the people willingly offer themselves,
Bless the LORD!
Hear, O kings! Give ear, O princes!
I, even I, will sing to the LORD;
I will sing praise to the LORD God of Israel.
LORD, when You went out from Seir,
When You marched from the field of Edom,
The earth trembled and the heavens poured,
The clouds also poured water;
The mountains gushed before the LORD,
This Sinai, before the LORD God of Israel."

Judges 5:1–5

"Awake, awake, Deborah!
Awake, awake, sing a song!
Arise, Barak, and lead your captives away,
O son of Abinoam!"

Judges 5:12

Hagar

(Prayer for the Life of Her Child)

Then she went and sat down across from him at a distance of about a bowshot; for she said to herself, "Let me not see the death of the boy." So she sat opposite him, and lifted her voice and wept.

And God heard the voice of the lad. Then the angel of God called to Hagar out of heaven, and said to her, "What ails you, Hagar? Fear not, for God has heard the voice of the lad where he is.

"Arise, lift up the lad and hold him with your hand, for I will make him a great nation."

Then God opened her eyes, and she saw a well of water. And she went and filled the skin with water, and gave the lad a drink.

Genesis 21:16–19

Hannah

(Prayer to Heal Her Barrenness and to Give Her a Son)

And she was in bitterness of soul, and prayed to the LORD and wept in anguish.

Then she made a vow and said, "O LORD of hosts, if You will indeed look on the affliction of Your maidservant and remember me, and not forget Your maidservant, but will give Your maidservant a male child, then I will give him to the LORD all the days of his life, and no razor shall come upon his head."

I Samuel 1:10–11

"For this child I prayed, and the LORD has granted me my petition which I asked of Him.

"Therefore I also have lent him to the LORD; as long as he lives he shall be lent to the LORD." So they worshiped the LORD there.

I Samuel 1:27–28

(Prayer of Praise)

And Hannah prayed and said:
"My heart rejoices in the LORD;
My horn is exalted in the LORD.

I smile at my enemies,
Because I rejoice in Your salvation.
No one is holy like the LORD,
For there is none besides You,
Nor is there any rock like our God.
Talk no more so very proudly;
Let no arrogance come from your mouth,
For the LORD is the God of knowledge;
And by Him actions are weighed.
The bows of the mighty men are broken,
And those who stumbled are girded with strength.
Those who were full have hired themselves out
for bread,
And the hungry have ceased to hunger.
Even the barren has borne seven,
And she who has many children has become feeble.
The LORD kills and makes alive;
He brings down to the grave and brings up.
The LORD makes poor and makes rich;
He brings low and lifts up.
He raises the poor from the dust
And lifts the beggar from the ash heap,
To set them among princes
And make them inherit the throne of glory.
For the pillars of the earth are the LORD'S,
And He has set the world upon them.
He will guard the feet of His saints,

But the wicked shall be silent in darkness.
For by strength no man shall prevail.
The adversaries of the LORD shall be broken in pieces;
From heaven He will thunder against them.
The LORD will judge the ends of the earth.
He will give strength to His king,
And exalt the horn of His anointed."

I Samuel 2:1–10

Leah

❧

(Prayer of Praise for Her Children)

So Leah conceived and bore a son, and she called his name Reuben; for she said, "The LORD has surely looked on my affliction. Now therefore, my husband will love me."

Then she conceived again and bore a son, and said, "Because the LORD has heard that I am unloved, He has therefore given me this son also." And she called his name Simeon.

She conceived again and bore a son, and said, "Now this time my husband will become attached to me, because I have borne him three sons." Therefore his name was called Levi.

And she conceived again and bore a son, and said, "Now I will praise the LORD." Therefore she called his name Judah. Then she stopped bearing.

Genesis 29:32–35

Mary

(Prayer of Praise)

And Mary said:
"My soul magnifies the Lord,
And my spirit has rejoiced in God my Savior.
For He has regarded the lowly state of His
maidservant;
For behold, henceforth all generations will call
me blessed.
For He who is mighty has done great things for me,
And holy is His name.
And His mercy is on those who fear Him
From generation to generation.
He has shown strength with His arm;
He has scattered the proud in the imagination of
their hearts.
He has put down the mighty from their thrones,
And exalted the lowly.
He has filled the hungry with good things,
And the rich He has sent away empty."

Luke 1:46–53

Naomi

(Prayer for Rest and Marriage for Daughters-in-Law)

And Naomi said to her two daughters-in-law, "Go, return each to her mother's house. The LORD deal kindly with you, as you have dealt with the dead and with me.

"The LORD grant that you may find rest, each in the house of her husband." So she kissed them, and they lifted up their voices and wept.

Ruth 1:8–9

Then Naomi said to her daughter-in-law, "Blessed be he of the LORD, who has not forsaken His kindness to the living and the dead!" And Naomi said to her, "This man is a relation of ours, one of our close relatives."

Ruth 2:20

Rachel

❦

(Prayer to Bear a Child)

Now when Rachel saw that she bore Jacob no children, Rachel envied her sister, and said to Jacob, "Give me children, or else I die!"

And Jacob's anger was aroused against Rachel, and he said, "Am I in the place of God, who has withheld from you the fruit of the womb?"

Then God remembered Rachel, and God listened to her and opened her womb.

And she conceived and bore a son, and said, "God has taken away my reproach."

So she called his name Joseph, and said, "The LORD shall add to me another son."

Genesis 30:1–2, 22–24

Shunammite Mother
❦
(Prayer for a Child)

Now it happened one day that Elisha went to Shunem, where there was a notable woman, and she persuaded him to eat some food. So it was, as often as he passed by, he would turn in there to eat some food.

And she said to her husband, "Look now, I know that this is a holy man of God, who passes by us regularly.

"Please, let us make a small upper room on the wall; and let us put a bed for him there, and a table and a chair and a lampstand; so it will be, whenever he comes to us, he can turn in there."

And it happened one day that he came there, and he turned in to the upper room and lay down there.

Then he said to Gehazi his servant, "Call this Shunammite woman." When he had called her, she stood before him.

And he said to him, "Say now to her, 'Look, you have been concerned for us with all this care. What can I do for you? Do you want me to speak on your behalf to the king or to the commander of the army?'" She answered, "I dwell among my own people."

So he said, "What then is to be done for her?" And Gehazi answered, "Actually, she has no son, and her husband is old."

So he said, "Call her." When he had called her, she stood in the doorway.

Then he said, "About this time next year you shall embrace a son." And she said, "No, my lord. Man of God, do not lie to your maidservant!"

But the woman conceived, and bore a son when the appointed time had come, of which Elisha had told her.

II Kings 4:8–17

(Prayer for Resurrection of Her Child)

And the child grew. Now it happened one day that he went out to his father, to the reapers.

And he said to his father, "My head, my head!" So he said to a servant, "Carry him to his mother."

When he had taken him and brought him to his mother, he sat on her knees till noon, and then died.

When Elisha came into the house, there was the child, lying dead on his bed.

He went in therefore, shut the door behind the two of them, and prayed to the LORD.

And he went up and lay on the child, and put his mouth on his mouth, his eyes on his eyes, and his hands on his hands; and he stretched himself out on the child, and the flesh of the child became warm.

II Kings 4:18–20, 32–34

Syrophoenician Mother

❧

(Prayer for Deliverance of
Demon-Possessed Daughter)

And behold, a woman of Canaan came from that region and cried out to Him, saying, "Have mercy on me, O Lord, Son of David! My daughter is severely demon-possessed."

But He answered her not a word. And His disciples came and urged Him, saying, "Send her away, for she cries out after us."

But He answered and said, "I was not sent except to the lost sheep of the house of Israel."

Then she came and worshiped Him, saying, "Lord, help me!"

But He answered and said, "It is not good to take the children's bread and throw it to the little dogs."

And she said, "Yes, Lord, yet even the little dogs eat the crumbs which fall from their masters' table."

Then Jesus answered and said to her, "O woman, great is your faith! Let it be to you as you desire." And her daughter was healed from that very hour.

Matthew 15:22–28

Widow with Two Sons

(Prayer for Finances to Save Household and Sons)

So Elisha said to her, "What shall I do for you? Tell me, what do you have in the house?" And she said, "Your maidservant has nothing in the house but a jar of oil."

Then he said, "Go, borrow vessels from everywhere, from all your neighbors—empty vessels; do not gather just a few.

"And when you have come in, you shall shut the door behind you and your sons; then pour it into all those vessels, and set aside the full ones."

So she went from him and shut the door behind her and her sons, who brought the vessels to her; and she poured it out.

Now it came to pass, when the vessels were full, that she said to her son, "Bring me another vessel." And he said to her, "There is not another vessel." So the oil ceased.

Then she came and told the man of God. And he said, "Go, sell the oil and pay your debt; and you and your sons live on the rest."

II Kings 4:2–7

Zarephath Widow

❀

(Prayer for Resurrection of Dead Son)

Now it happened after these things that the son of the woman who owned the house became sick. And his sickness was so serious that there was no breath left in him.

So she said to Elijah, "What have I to do with you, O man of God? Have you come to me to bring my sin to remembrance, and to kill my son?"

And he said to her, "Give me your son." So he took him out of her arms and carried him to the upper room where he was staying, and laid him on his own bed.

Then he cried out to the LORD and said, "O LORD my God, have You also brought tragedy on the widow with whom I lodge, by killing her son?"

And he stretched himself out on the child three times, and cried out to the LORD and said, "O LORD my God, I pray, let this child's soul come back to him."

Then the LORD heard the voice of Elijah; and the soul of the child came back to him, and he revived.

I Kings 17:17–22

The Responsibilities
of Motherhood

Commitment

"Can a woman forget her nursing child,
And not have compassion on the son of her womb?
Surely they may forget,
Yet I will not forget you.
See, I have inscribed you on the palms of My hands;
Your walls are continually before Me."

Isaiah 49:15–16

And the mother of the child said, "As the LORD lives, and as your soul lives, I will not leave you." So he arose and followed her.

II Kings 4:30

She considers a field and buys it;
From her profits she plants a vineyard.

Proverbs 31:16

Then she said to him, "My lord, you swore by the LORD your God to your maidservant, saying, 'Assuredly Solomon your son shall reign after me, and he shall sit on my throne.'"

I Kings 1:17

Compassion

❧

And when she opened it, she saw the child, and behold, the baby wept. So she had compassion on him, and said, "This is one of the Hebrews' children."

Then his sister said to Pharaoh's daughter, "Shall I go and call a nurse for you from the Hebrew women, that she may nurse the child for you?"

And Pharaoh's daughter said to her, "Go." So the maiden went and called the child's mother.

Then Pharaoh's daughter said to her, "Take this child away and nurse him for me, and I will give you your wages." So the woman took the child and nursed him.

And the child grew, and she brought him to Pharaoh's daughter, and he became her son. So she called his name Moses, saying, "Because I drew him out of the water."

Exodus 2:6–10

She extends her hand to the poor,
Yes, she reaches out her hands to the needy.

Proverbs 31:20

"Can a woman forget her nursing child,
And not have compassion on the son of her womb?

Surely they may forget,
Yet I will not forget you."

Isaiah 49:15

"As one whom his mother comforts,
So I will comfort you;
And you shall be comforted in Jerusalem."

Isaiah 66:13

Then Isaac brought her into his mother Sarah's tent; and he took Rebekah and she became his wife, and he loved her. So Isaac was comforted after his mother's death.

Genesis 24:67

Discipline

❦

Do not withhold correction from a child,
For if you beat him with a rod, he will not die.
You shall beat him with a rod,
And deliver his soul from hell.

Proverbs 23:13–14

The rod and rebuke give wisdom,
But a child left to himself brings shame to his mother.
Correct your son, and he will give you rest;
Yes, he will give delight to your soul.

Proverbs 29:15, 17

She girds herself with strength,
And strengthens her arms.
She perceives that her merchandise is good,
And her lamp does not go out by night.
She watches over the ways of her household,
And does not eat the bread of idleness.

Proverbs 31:17–18, 27

The Angel of the LORD said to her, "Return to your
mistress, and submit yourself under her hand."

Genesis 16:9

Example
❧

Strength and honor are her clothing;
She shall rejoice in time to come.

Proverbs 31:25

"Now therefore, please be careful not to drink wine or similar drink, and not to eat anything unclean.

"For behold, you shall conceive and bear a son. And no razor shall come upon his head, for the child shall be a Nazirite to God from the womb; and he shall begin to deliver Israel out of the hand of the Philistines."

"And He said to me, 'Behold, you shall conceive and bear a son. Now drink no wine or similar drink, nor eat anything unclean, for the child shall be a Nazirite to God from the womb to the day of his death.'"

Judges 13:4–5, 7

That the older men be sober, reverent, temperate, sound in faith, in love, in patience;

the older women likewise, that they be reverent in behavior, not slanderers, not given to much wine, teachers of good things—

that they admonish the young women to love their husbands, to love their children,

to be discreet, chaste, homemakers, good, obedient

to their own husbands, that the word of God may not be blasphemed.

In all things showing yourself to be a pattern of good works; in doctrine showing integrity, reverence, incorruptibility.

Titus 2:2–5, 7

But if any widow has children or grandchildren, let them first learn to show piety at home and to repay their parents; for this is good and acceptable before God.

Now she who is really a widow, and left alone, trusts in God and continues in supplications and prayers night and day.

But she who lives in pleasure is dead while she lives.

I Timothy 5:4–6

Faith

❧

But when she could no longer hide him, she took an ark of bulrushes for him, daubed it with asphalt and pitch, put the child in it, and laid it in the reeds by the river's bank.

Exodus 2:3

Then Jesus answered and said to her, "O woman, great is your faith! Let it be to you as you desire." And her daughter was healed from that very hour.

Matthew 15:28

"The LORD repay your work, and a full reward be given you by the LORD God of Israel, under whose wings you have come for refuge."

Ruth 2:12

Godliness

❧

And it happened, when Elizabeth heard the greeting of Mary, that the babe leaped in her womb; and Elizabeth was filled with the Holy Spirit.

Luke 1:41

Charm is deceitful and beauty is passing,
But a woman who fears the LORD, she shall be
praised.

Proverbs 31:30

Who can find a virtuous wife?
For her worth is far above rubies.
The heart of her husband safely trusts her;
So he will have no lack of gain.
She does him good and not evil
All the days of her life.

Proverbs 31:10–12

But, which is proper for women professing godliness, with good works.

I Timothy 2:10

But reject profane and old wives' fables, and exercise yourself toward godliness.

I Timothy 4:7

Home

❧

To be discreet, chaste, homemakers, good, obedient to their own husbands, that the word of God may not be blasphemed.

Titus 2:5

She watches over the ways of her household,
And does not eat the bread of idleness.

Proverbs 31:27

Then He said to the disciple, "Behold your mother!" And from that hour that disciple took her to his own home.

John 19:27

But if any widow has children or grandchildren, let them first learn to show piety at home and to repay their parents; for this is good and acceptable before God.

I Timothy 5:4

Intercession

❧

And He said to her, "What do you wish?" She said to Him, "Grant that these two sons of mine may sit, one on Your right hand and the other on the left, in Your kingdom."

Matthew 20:21

Then she said to him, "My lord, you swore by the LORD your God to your maidservant, saying, 'Assuredly Solomon your son shall reign after me, and he shall sit on my throne.'"

I Kings 1:17

And behold, a woman of Canaan came from that region and cried out to Him, saying, "Have mercy on me, O Lord, Son of David! My daughter is severely demon-possessed."

But He answered her not a word. And His disciples came and urged Him, saying, "Send her away, for she cries out after us."

But He answered and said, "I was not sent except to the lost sheep of the house of Israel."

Then she came and worshiped Him, saying, "Lord, help me!"

But He answered and said, "It is not good to take the children's bread and throw it to the little dogs."

And she said, "Yes, Lord, yet even the little dogs eat the crumbs which fall from their masters' table."

Then Jesus answered and said to her, "O woman, great is your faith! Let it be to you as you desire." And her daughter was healed from that very hour.

Matthew 15:22–28

And Elijah said to her, "Do not fear; go and do as you have said, but make me a small cake from it first, and bring it to me; and afterward make some for yourself and your son.

"For thus says the LORD God of Israel: 'The bin of flour shall not be used up, nor shall the jar of oil run dry, until the day the LORD sends rain on the earth.'"

I Kings 17:13–14

Love

That they admonish the young women to love their husbands, to love their children.

Titus 2:4

I rejoiced greatly that I have found some of your children walking in truth, as we received commandment from the Father.

And now I plead with you, lady, not as though I wrote a new commandment to you, but that which we have had from the beginning: that we love one another.

II John 1:4–5

Morality

❧

And they were both righteous before God, walking in all the commandments and ordinances of the Lord blameless.

Luke 1:6

Who can find a virtuous wife?
For her worth is far above rubies.
The heart of her husband safely trusts her;
So he will have no lack of gain.

Proverbs 31:10–11

To be discreet, chaste, homemakers, good, obedient to their own husbands, that the word of God may not be blasphemed.

Titus 2:5

"Many daughters have done well,
But you excel them all."

Proverbs 31:29

Now therefore, please be careful not to drink wine or similar drink, and not to eat anything unclean.

Judges 13:4

Obedience

❧

Then Mary said, "Behold the maidservant of the Lord! Let it be to me according to your word." And the angel departed from her.

Luke 1:38

When the morning dawned, the angels urged Lot to hurry, saying, "Arise, take your wife and your two daughters who are here, lest you be consumed in the punishment of the city."

Genesis 19:15

But his wife looked back behind him, and she became a pillar of salt.

Genesis 19:26

"Remember Lot's wife.
"Whoever seeks to save his life will lose it, and whoever loses his life will preserve it."

Luke 17:32–33

So Noah, with his sons, his wife, and his sons' wives, went into the ark because of the waters of the flood.

Genesis 7:7

And Elijah said to her, "Do not fear; go and do as you have said, but make me a small cake from it first, and bring it to me; and afterward make some for yourself and your son."

I Kings 17:13

So she went away and did according to the word of Elijah; and she and he and her household ate for many days.

I Kings 17:15

Then she said to him, "My lord, you swore by the LORD your God to your maidservant, saying, 'Assuredly Solomon your son shall reign after me, and he shall sit on my throne.'"

I Kings 1:17

As Sarah obeyed Abraham, calling him lord, whose daughters you are if you do good and are not afraid with any terror.

I Peter 3:6

Prayer

Then she went and sat down across from him at a distance of about a bowshot; for she said to herself, "Let me not see the death of the boy." So she sat opposite him, and lifted her voice and wept.

Genesis 21:16

And she was in bitterness of soul, and prayed to the LORD and wept in anguish.

Then she made a vow and said, "O LORD of hosts, if You will indeed look on the affliction of Your maidservant and remember me, and not forget Your maidservant, but will give Your maidservant a male child, then I will give him to the LORD all the days of his life, and no razor shall come upon his head."

And it happened, as she continued praying before the LORD, that Eli watched her mouth.

I Samuel 1:10–12

So it came to pass in the process of time that Hannah conceived and bore a son, and called his name Samuel, saying, "Because I have asked for him from the LORD."

I Samuel 1:20

And behold, a woman of Canaan came from that region and cried out to Him, saying, "Have mercy on me, O Lord, Son of David! My daughter is severely demon-possessed."

But He answered her not a word. And His disciples came and urged Him, saying, "Send her away, for she cries out after us."

But He answered and said, "I was not sent except to the lost sheep of the house of Israel."

Then she came and worshiped Him, saying, "Lord, help me!"

But He answered and said, "It is not good to take the children's bread and throw it to the little dogs."

And she said, "Yes, Lord, yet even the little dogs eat the crumbs which fall from their masters' table."

Then Jesus answered and said to her, "O woman, great is your faith! Let it be to you as you desire." And her daughter was healed from that very hour.

Matthew 15:22–28

"For this child I prayed, and the LORD has granted me my petition which I asked of Him.

"Therefore I also have lent him to the LORD; as long as he lives he shall be lent to the LORD." So they worshiped the LORD there.

I Samuel 1:27–28

The Responsibilities of Motherhood

Provision

❦

Moreover his mother used to make him a little robe, and bring it to him year by year when she came up with her husband to offer the yearly sacrifice.

I Samuel 2:19

And she brought forth her firstborn Son, and wrapped Him in swaddling cloths, and laid Him in a manger, because there was no room for them in the inn.

Luke 2:7

She considers a field and buys it;
From her profits she plants a vineyard.

Proverbs 31:16

But when she could no longer hide him, she took an ark of bulrushes for him, daubed it with asphalt and pitch, put the child in it, and laid it in the reeds by the river's bank.

And his sister stood afar off, to know what would be done to him.

Exodus 2:3–4

Sacrifice

❧

And she was in bitterness of soul, and prayed to the LORD and wept in anguish.

Then she made a vow and said, "O LORD of hosts, if You will indeed look on the affliction of Your maidservant and remember me, and not forget Your maidservant, but will give Your maidservant a male child, then I will give him to the LORD all the days of his life, and no razor shall come upon his head."

I Samuel 1:10–11

But Hannah did not go up, for she said to her husband, "Not until the child is weaned; then I will take him, that he may appear before the LORD and remain there forever."

So Elkanah her husband said to her, "Do what seems best to you; wait until you have weaned him. Only let the LORD establish His word." Then the woman stayed and nursed her son until she had weaned him.

Now when she had weaned him, she took him up with her, with three bulls, one ephah of flour, and a skin of wine, and brought him to the house of the LORD in Shiloh. And the child was young.

Then they slaughtered a bull, and brought the child to Eli.

And she said, "O my lord! As your soul lives, my lord, I am the woman who stood by you here, praying to the LORD.

"For this child I prayed, and the LORD has granted me my petition which I asked of Him.

"Therefore I also have lent him to the LORD; as long as he lives he shall be lent to the LORD." So they worshiped the LORD there.

I Samuel 1:22–28

To the woman He said:
"I will greatly multiply your sorrow and your
     conception;
In pain you shall bring forth children;
Your desire shall be for your husband,
And he shall rule over you."

Genesis 3:16

Wives, submit to your own husbands, as is fitting in the Lord.

Colossians 3:18

Then Mary said, "Behold the maidservant of the Lord! Let it be to me according to your word." And the angel departed from her.

Luke 1:38

Wives, likewise, be submissive to your own husbands, that even if some do not obey the word, they, without a word, may be won by the conduct of their wives.

I Peter 3:1

Thankfulness

❦

So she went in, fell at his feet, and bowed to the ground; then she picked up her son and went out.

II Kings 4:37

Then Bathsheba bowed with her face to the earth, and paid homage to the king, and said, "Let my lord King David live forever!"

I Kings 1:31

And Hannah prayed and said:
"My heart rejoices in the LORD;
My horn is exalted in the LORD.
I smile at my enemies,
Because I rejoice in Your salvation."

I Samuel 2:1

Then Naomi said to her daughter-in-law, "Blessed be he of the LORD, who has not forsaken His kindness to the living and the dead!" And Naomi said to her, "This man is a relation of ours, one of our close relatives."

Ruth 2:20

And Mary said:
"My soul magnifies the Lord,
And my spirit has rejoiced in God my Savior.
For He has regarded the lowly state of His
maidservant;
For behold, henceforth all generations will call
me blessed.
For He who is mighty has done great things for me,
And holy is His name.
And His mercy is on those who fear Him
From generation to generation.
He has shown strength with His arm;
He has scattered the proud in the imagination of
their hearts.
He has put down the mighty from their thrones,
And exalted the lowly.
He has filled the hungry with good things,
And the rich He has sent away empty."

Luke 1:46–53

The Promises
of Motherhood

Abundance

And Leah said, "God has endowed me with a good endowment; now my husband will dwell with me, because I have borne him six sons." So she called his name Zebulun.

Genesis 30:20

And when they had come into the house, they saw the young Child with Mary His mother, and fell down and worshiped Him. And when they had opened their treasures, they presented gifts to Him: gold, frankincense, and myrrh.

Matthew 2:11

And they blessed Rebekah and said to her:
"Our sister, may you become
The mother of thousands of ten thousands;
And may your descendants possess
The gates of those who hate them."

Genesis 24:60

The bin of flour was not used up, nor did the jar of oil run dry, according to the word of the LORD which He spoke by Elijah.

I Kings 17:16

Compassion

❦

When the LORD saw that Leah was unloved, He opened her womb; but Rachel was barren.

So Leah conceived and bore a son, and she called his name Reuben; for she said, "The LORD has surely looked on my affliction. Now therefore, my husband will love me."

Then she conceived again and bore a son, and said, "Because the LORD has heard that I am unloved, He has therefore given me this son also." And she called his name Simeon.

She conceived again and bore a son, and said, "Now this time my husband will become attached to me, because I have borne him three sons." Therefore his name was called Levi.

Genesis 29:31–34

When the Lord saw her, He had compassion on her and said to her, "Do not weep."

Then He came and touched the open coffin, and those who carried him stood still. And He said, "Young man, I say to you, arise."

So he who was dead sat up and began to speak. And He presented him to his mother.

Then fear came upon all, and they glorified God, saying, "A great prophet has risen up among us"; and, "God has visited His people."

Luke 7:13–16

Through the LORD'S mercies we are not consumed,
Because His compassions fail not.
They are new every morning;
Great is Your faithfulness.
"The LORD is my portion," says my soul,
"Therefore I hope in Him!"

Lamentations 3:22–24

"Can a woman forget her nursing child,
And not have compassion on the son of her womb?
Surely they may forget,
Yet I will not forget you.
See, I have inscribed you on the palms of My hands
Your walls are continually before Me."

Isaiah 49:15–16

Fruitfulness

❦

And it happened, when Elizabeth heard the greeting of Mary, that the babe leaped in her womb; and Elizabeth was filled with the Holy Spirit.

Then she spoke out with a loud voice and said, "Blessed are you among women, and blessed is the fruit of your womb!

"But why is this granted to me, that the mother of my Lord should come to me?

"For indeed, as soon as the voice of your greeting sounded in my ears, the babe leaped in my womb for joy.

"Blessed is she who believed, for there will be a fulfillment of those things which were told her from the Lord."

Luke 1:41–45

And the LORD visited Sarah as He had said, and the LORD did for Sarah as He had spoken.

For Sarah conceived and bore Abraham a son in his old age, at the set time of which God had spoken to him.

And Abraham called the name of his son who was born to him—whom Sarah bore to him—Isaac.

Genesis 21:1–3

So it was, that while they were there, the days were completed for her to be delivered.

And she brought forth her firstborn Son, and wrapped Him in swaddling cloths, and laid Him in a manger, because there was no room for them in the inn.

Luke 2:6–7

Then she spoke out with a loud voice and said, "Blessed are you among women, and blessed is the fruit of your womb!"

Luke 1:42

And the LORD visited Hannah, so that she conceived and bore three sons and two daughters. Meanwhile the child Samuel grew before the LORD.

I Samuel 2:21

So she called his name Joseph, and said, "The LORD shall add to me another son."

Genesis 30:24

Your wife shall be like a fruitful vine
In the very heart of your house,
Your children like olive plants
All around your table.

Psalm 128:3

Grace

But when it pleased God, who separated me from my mother's womb and called me through His grace.

Galatians 1:15

When the LORD saw that Leah was unloved, He opened her womb; but Rachel was barren.

So Leah conceived and bore a son, and she called his name Reuben; for she said, "The LORD has surely looked on my affliction. Now therefore, my husband will love me."

Genesis 29:31–32

Nevertheless she will be saved in childbearing if they continue in faith, love, and holiness, with self-control.

I Timothy 2:15

"And His mercy is on those who fear Him
From generation to generation."

Luke 1:50

When the Lord saw her, He had compassion on her and said to her, "Do not weep."

Luke 7:13

Guidance

❧

"They shall neither hunger nor thirst,
Neither heat nor sun shall strike them;
For He who has mercy on them will lead them,
Even by the springs of water He will guide them.
I will make each of My mountains a road,
And My highways shall be elevated."

Isaiah 49:10–11

Saying, "Arise, take the young Child and His mother,
and go to the land of Israel, for those who sought the
young Child's life are dead."
Then he arose, took the young Child and His
mother, and came into the land of Israel.

Matthew 2:20–21

"(But from my youth I reared him as a father,
And from my mother's womb I guided the widow.)"

Job 31:18

Your ears shall hear a word behind you, saying,
"This is the way, walk in it,"
Whenever you turn to the right hand
Or whenever you turn to the left.

Isaiah 30:21

"The LORD will guide you continually,
And satisfy your soul in drought,
And strengthen your bones;
You shall be like a watered garden,
And like a spring of water, whose waters do not fail."

Isaiah 58:11

For this is God,
Our God forever and ever;
He will be our guide
Even to death.

Psalm 48:14

"For the Holy Spirit will teach you in that very hour
what you ought to say."

Luke 12:12

Honor

❧

"And now, my daughter, do not fear. I will do for you all that you request, for all the people of my town know that you are a virtuous woman."

Ruth 3:11

A gracious woman retains honor,
But ruthless men retain riches.

Proverbs 11:16

And Mary said:
"My soul magnifies the Lord,
And my spirit has rejoiced in God my Savior.
For He has regarded the lowly state of His
maidservant;
For behold, henceforth all generations will call
me blessed.
For He who is mighty has done great things for me,
And holy is His name.
And His mercy is on those who fear Him
From generation to generation.
He has shown strength with His arm;
He has scattered the proud in the imagination of
their hearts.

He has put down the mighty from their thrones,
And exalted the lowly.
He has filled the hungry with good things,
And the rich He has sent away empty.
He has helped His servant Israel,
In remembrance of His mercy,
As He spoke to our fathers,
To Abraham and to his seed forever."

Luke 1:46–55

"Honor your father and your mother, that your days may be long upon the land which the LORD your God is giving you."

Exodus 20:12

"'Honor your father and your mother,' and, 'You shall love your neighbor as yourself.'"

Matthew 19:19

Joy

"For indeed, as soon as the voice of your greeting sounded in my ears, the babe leaped in my womb for joy.

"Blessed is she who believed, for there will be a fulfillment of those things which were told her from the Lord."

Luke 1:44–45

"And you will have joy and gladness, and many will rejoice at his birth."

Luke 1:14

And Mary said:
"My soul magnifies the Lord,
And my spirit has rejoiced in God my Savior.
For He has regarded the lowly state of His
maidservant;
For behold, henceforth all generations will call
me blessed.
For He who is mighty has done great things for me,
And holy is His name."

Luke 1:46–49

He grants the barren woman a home,
Like a joyful mother of children.
Praise the LORD!

Psalm 113:9

Let your father and your mother be glad,
And let her who bore you rejoice.

Proverbs 23:25

This is the day the LORD has made;
We will rejoice and be glad in it.

Psalm 118:24

Her children rise up and call her blessed;
Her husband also, and he praises her:
"Many daughters have done well,
But you excel them all."
Charm is deceitful and beauty is passing,
But a woman who fears the LORD, she shall be praised.
Give her of the fruit of her hands,
And let her own works praise her in the gates.

Proverbs 31:28–31

Love

And when she rose up to glean, Boaz commanded his young men, saying, "Let her glean even among the sheaves, and do not reproach her.

"Also let grain from the bundles fall purposely for her; leave it that she may glean, and do not rebuke her."

Ruth 2:15–16

So Boaz took Ruth and she became his wife; and when he went in to her, the LORD gave her conception, and she bore a son.

Ruth 4:13

Then Isaac brought her into his mother Sarah's tent; and he took Rebekah and she became his wife, and he loved her. So Isaac was comforted after his mother's death.

Genesis 24:67

Now Jacob loved Rachel; so he said, "I will serve you seven years for Rachel your younger daughter."

So Jacob served seven years for Rachel, and they seemed only a few days to him because of the love he had for her.

Genesis 29:18, 20

Prosperity

"But every woman shall ask of her neighbor, namely, of her who dwells near her house, articles of silver, articles of gold, and clothing; and you shall put them on your sons and on your daughters. So you shall plunder the Egyptians."

Exodus 3:22

So Elisha said to her, "What shall I do for you? Tell me, what do you have in the house?" And she said, "Your maidservant has nothing in the house but a jar of oil."

Then he said, "Go, borrow vessels from everywhere, from all your neighbors—empty vessels; do not gather just a few.

"And when you have come in, you shall shut the door behind you and your sons; then pour it into all those vessels, and set aside the full ones."

So she went from him and shut the door behind her and her sons, who brought the vessels to her; and she poured it out.

Now it came to pass, when the vessels were full, that she said to her son, "Bring me another vessel." And he said to her, "There is not another vessel." So the oil ceased.

Then she came and told the man of God. And he

said, "Go, sell the oil and pay your debt; and you and your sons live on the rest."

II Kings 4:2–7

"For thus says the LORD God of Israel: 'The bin of flour shall not be used up, nor shall the jar of oil run dry, until the day the LORD sends rain on the earth.'"

So she went away and did according to the word of Elijah; and she and he and her household ate for many days.

The bin of flour was not used up, nor did the jar of oil run dry, according to the word of the LORD which He spoke by Elijah.

I Kings 17:14–16

Protection

❧

But when she could no longer hide him, she took an ark of bulrushes for him, daubed it with asphalt and pitch, put the child in it, and laid it in the reeds by the river's bank.

And his sister stood afar off, to know what would be done to him.

Then the daughter of Pharaoh came down to bathe at the river. And her maidens walked along the riverside; and when she saw the ark among the reeds, she sent her maid to get it.

And when she opened it, she saw the child, and behold, the baby wept. So she had compassion on him, and said, "This is one of the Hebrews' children."

Exodus 2:3–6

So Noah, with his sons, his wife, and his sons' wives, went into the ark because of the waters of the flood.

And the waters prevailed on the earth one hundred and fifty days.

Genesis 7:7, 24

"If men fight, and hurt a woman with child, so that she gives birth prematurely, yet no harm follows, he shall surely be punished accordingly as the woman's husband imposes on him; and he shall pay as the judges determine."

Exodus 21:22

But the Lord is faithful, who will establish you and guard you from the evil one.

II Thessalonians 3:3

Provision

❧

Listen to your father who begot you,
And do not despise your mother when she is old.

Proverbs 23:22

Now there stood by the cross of Jesus His mother, and His mother's sister, Mary the wife of Clopas, and Mary Magdalene.

When Jesus therefore saw His mother, and the disciple whom He loved standing by, He said to His mother, "Woman, behold your son!"

Then He said to the disciple, "Behold your mother!" And from that hour that disciple took her to his own home.

John 19:25–27

Then, being divinely warned in a dream that they should not return to Herod, they departed for their own country another way.

Now when they had departed, behold, an angel of the Lord appeared to Joseph in a dream, saying, "Arise, take the young Child and His mother, flee to Egypt, and stay there until I bring you word; for Herod will seek the young Child to destroy Him."

When he arose, he took the young Child and His mother by night and departed for Egypt,

and was there until the death of Herod, that it might be fulfilled which was spoken by the Lord through the prophet, saying, "Out of Egypt I called My Son."

Matthew 2:12–15

A certain woman of the wives of the sons of the prophets cried out to Elisha, saying, "Your servant my husband is dead, and you know that your servant feared the LORD. And the creditor is coming to take my two sons to be his slaves."

So Elisha said to her, "What shall I do for you? Tell me, what do you have in the house?" And she said, "Your maidservant has nothing in the house but a jar of oil."

Then he said, "Go, borrow vessels from everywhere, from all your neighbors—empty vessels; do not gather just a few.

"And when you have come in, you shall shut the door behind you and your sons; then pour it into all those vessels, and set aside the full ones."

So she went from him and shut the door behind her and her sons, who brought the vessels to her; and she poured it out.

Now it came to pass, when the vessels were full, that she said to her son, "Bring me another vessel." And he said to her, "There is not another vessel." So the oil ceased.

Then she came and told the man of God. And he said, "Go, sell the oil and pay your debt; and you and your sons live on the rest."

II Kings 4:1–7

"Arise, lift up the lad and hold him with your hand, for I will make him a great nation."

Then God opened her eyes, and she saw a well of water. And she went and filled the skin with water, and gave the lad a drink.

Genesis 21:18–19

Respect

❧

'Every one of you shall revere his mother and his father, and keep My Sabbaths: I am the LORD your God.'

Leviticus 19:3

My son, hear the instruction of your father,
And do not forsake the law of your mother;
For they will be a graceful ornament on your head,
And chains about your neck.

Proverbs 1:8–9

My son, keep your father's command,
And do not forsake the law of your mother.
Bind them continually upon your heart;
Tie them around your neck.
When you roam, they will lead you;
When you sleep, they will keep you;
And when you awake, they will speak with you.

Proverbs 6:20–22

Whoever curses his father or his mother,
His lamp will be put out in deep darkness.

Proverbs 20:20

Resurrection

❧

Now it happened, the day after, that He went into a city called Nain; and many of His disciples went with Him, and a large crowd.

And when He came near the gate of the city, behold, a dead man was being carried out, the only son of his mother; and she was a widow. And a large crowd from the city was with her.

When the Lord saw her, He had compassion on her and said to her, "Do not weep."

Then He came and touched the open coffin, and those who carried him stood still. And He said, "Young man, I say to you, arise."

So he who was dead sat up and began to speak. And He presented him to his mother.

Then fear came upon all, and they glorified God, saying, "A great prophet has risen up among us"; and, "God has visited His people."

And this report about Him went throughout all Judea and all the surrounding region.

Luke 7:11–17

When Elisha came into the house, there was the child, lying dead on his bed.

He went in therefore, shut the door behind the two of them, and prayed to the LORD.

And he went up and lay on the child, and put his mouth on his mouth, his eyes on his eyes, and his hands on his hands; and he stretched himself out on the child, and the flesh of the child became warm.

He returned and walked back and forth in the house, and again went up and stretched himself out on him; then the child sneezed seven times, and the child opened his eyes.

And he called Gehazi and said, "Call this Shunammite woman." So he called her. And when she came in to him, he said, "Pick up your son."

So she went in, fell at his feet, and bowed to the ground; then she picked up her son and went out.

II Kings 4:32–37

Trust

"The LORD repay your work, and a full reward be given you by the LORD God of Israel, under whose wings you have come for refuge."

Then she said, "Let me find favor in your sight, my lord; for you have comforted me, and have spoken kindly to your maidservant, though I am not like one of your maidservants."

Ruth 2:12–13

In God (I will praise His word),
In God I have put my trust;
I will not fear.
What can flesh do to me?

Psalm 56:4

The heart of her husband safely trusts her;
So he will have no lack of gain.

Proverbs 31:11

Trust in the LORD, and do good;
Dwell in the land, and feed on His faithfulness.
Delight yourself also in the LORD,
And He shall give you the desires of your heart.

Psalm 37:3–4

For in this manner, in former times, the holy women who trusted in God also adorned themselves, being submissive to their own husbands.

I Peter 3:5

Commit your way to the LORD,
Trust also in Him,
And He shall bring it to pass.
He shall bring forth your righteousness as the light,
And your justice as the noonday.

Psalm 37:5–6

"Come to Me, all you who labor and are heavy laden, and I will give you rest.

"Take My yoke upon you and learn from Me, for I am gentle and lowly in heart, and you will find rest for your souls.

"For My yoke is easy and My burden is light."

Matthew 11:28–30

Cast your burden on the LORD,
And He shall sustain you;
He shall never permit the righteous to be moved.

Psalm 55:22

Understanding

❧

Discretion will preserve you;
Understanding will keep you,
To deliver you from the way of evil,
From the man who speaks perverse things.

Proverbs 2:11–12

Through wisdom a house is built,
And by understanding it is established;
By knowledge the rooms are filled
With all precious and pleasant riches.

Proverbs 24:3–4

And we know that the Son of God has come and has given us an understanding, that we may know Him who is true; and we are in Him who is true, in His Son Jesus Christ. This is the true God and eternal life.

I John 5:20

For in this manner, in former times, the holy women who trusted in God also adorned themselves, being submissive to their own husbands.

I Peter 3:5

Commit your way to the LORD,
Trust also in Him,

And He shall bring it to pass.
He shall bring forth your righteousness as the light,
And your justice as the noonday.

Psalm 37:5–6

"Come to Me, all you who labor and are heavy laden, and I will give you rest.

"Take My yoke upon you and learn from Me, for I am gentle and lowly in heart, and you will find rest for your souls.

"For My yoke is easy and My burden is light."

Matthew 11:28–30

Cast your burden on the LORD,
And He shall sustain you;
He shall never permit the righteous to be moved.

Psalm 55:22

The Blessings
of Motherhood

Angels

Now the Angel of the LORD found her by a spring of water in the wilderness, by the spring on the way to Shur.

And He said, "Hagar, Sarai's maid, where have you come from, and where are you going?" She said, "I am fleeing from the presence of my mistress Sarai."

The Angel of the LORD said to her, "Return to your mistress, and submit yourself under her hand."

Then the Angel of the LORD said to her, "I will multiply your descendants exceedingly, so that they shall not be counted for multitude."

And the Angel of the LORD said to her:
"Behold, you are with child,
And you shall bear a son.
You shall call his name Ishmael,
Because the LORD has heard your affliction."

Genesis 16:7–11

Now in the sixth month the angel Gabriel was sent by God to a city of Galilee named Nazareth,

to a virgin betrothed to a man whose name was Joseph, of the house of David. The virgin's name was Mary.

Luke 1:26–27

And God heard the voice of the lad. Then the angel of God called to Hagar out of heaven, and said to her, "What ails you, Hagar? Fear not, for God has heard the voice of the lad where he is."

Genesis 21:17

Again the children of Israel did evil in the sight of the LORD, and the LORD delivered them into the hand of the Philistines for forty years.

Now there was a certain man from Zorah, of the family of the Danites, whose name was Manoah; and his wife was barren and had no children.

And the Angel of the LORD appeared to the woman and said to her, "Indeed now, you are barren and have borne no children, but you shall conceive and bear a son.

"Now therefore, please be careful not to drink wine or similar drink, and not to eat anything unclean.

"For behold, you shall conceive and bear a son. And no razor shall come upon his head, for the child shall be a Nazirite to God from the womb; and he shall begin to deliver Israel out of the hand of the Philistines."

Judges 13:1–5

But the angel said to him, "Do not be afraid, Zacharias, for your prayer is heard; and your wife Elizabeth will bear you a son, and you shall call his name John."

Luke 1:13

Assurance

❦

"For thus says the LORD God of Israel: 'The bin of flour shall not be used up, nor shall the jar of oil run dry, until the day the LORD sends rain on the earth.'"

I Kings 17:14

Then David comforted Bathsheba his wife, and went in to her and lay with her. So she bore a son, and he called his name Solomon. Now the LORD loved him.

II Samuel 12:24

"Blessed are those who mourn,
For they shall be comforted."

Matthew 5:4

Then she said, "Let me find favor in your sight, my lord; for you have comforted me, and have spoken kindly to your maidservant, though I am not like one of your maidservants."

Ruth 2:13

And we know that all things work together for good to those who love God, to those who are the called according to His purpose.

Romans 8:28

Blessedness

❧

"And I will bless her and also give you a son by her; then I will bless her, and she shall be a mother of nations; kings of peoples shall be from her."

Then Abraham fell on his face and laughed, and said in his heart, "Shall a child be born to a man who is one hundred years old? And shall Sarah, who is ninety years old, bear a child?"

Genesis 17:16–17

And Jacob begot Joseph the husband of Mary, of whom was born Jesus who is called Christ.

So all the generations from Abraham to David are fourteen generations, from David until the captivity in Babylon are fourteen generations, and from the captivity in Babylon until the Christ are fourteen generations.

Now the birth of Jesus Christ was as follows: After His mother Mary was betrothed to Joseph, before they came together, she was found with child of the Holy Spirit.

Then Joseph her husband, being a just man, and not wanting to make her a public example, was minded to put her away secretly.

But while he thought about these things, behold, an

angel of the Lord appeared to him in a dream, saying, "Joseph, son of David, do not be afraid to take to you Mary your wife, for that which is conceived in her is of the Holy Spirit.

"And she will bring forth a Son, and you shall call His name JESUS, for He will save His people from their sins."

So all this was done that it might be fulfilled which was spoken by the Lord through the prophet, saying: "Behold, the virgin shall be with child, and bear a Son, and they shall call His name Immanuel," which is translated, "God with us."

Matthew 1:16–23

And it happened, as He spoke these things, that a certain woman from the crowd raised her voice and said to Him, "Blessed is the womb that bore You, and the breasts which nursed You!"

Luke 11:27

And having come in, the angel said to her, "Rejoice, highly favored one, the Lord is with you; blessed are you among women!"

But when she saw him, she was troubled at his saying, and considered what manner of greeting this was.

Then the angel said to her, "Do not be afraid, Mary, for you have found favor with God."

Luke 1:28–30

Then she spoke out with a loud voice and said, "Blessed are you among women, and blessed is the fruit of your womb!"

Luke 1:42

Children

❦

Now when Rachel saw that she bore Jacob no children, Rachel envied her sister, and said to Jacob, "Give me children, or else I die!"

And Jacob's anger was aroused against Rachel, and he said, "Am I in the place of God, who has withheld from you the fruit of the womb?"

Genesis 30:1–2

Now Adam knew Eve his wife, and she conceived and bore Cain, and said, "I have acquired a man from the LORD."

Genesis 4:1

Behold, children are a heritage from the LORD,
The fruit of the womb is a reward.

Psalm 127:3

"All your children shall be taught by the LORD,
And great shall be the peace of your children."

Isaiah 54:13

Contentment

Now godliness with contentment is great gain.

For we brought nothing into this world, and it is certain we can carry nothing out.

And having food and clothing, with these we shall be content.

I Timothy 6:6–8

"Therefore do not worry, saying, 'What shall we eat?' or 'What shall we drink?' or 'What shall we wear?'

"For after all these things the Gentiles seek. For your heavenly Father knows that you need all these things.

"But seek first the kingdom of God and His righteousness, and all these things shall be added to you.

"Therefore do not worry about tomorrow, for tomorrow will worry about its own things. Sufficient for the day is its own trouble."

Matthew 6:31–34

Let your conduct be without covetousness; be content with such things as you have. For He Himself has said, "I will never leave you nor forsake you."

So we may boldly say:

"The LORD is my helper;
I will not fear.
What can man do to me?"

Hebrews 13:5–6

Faith

❧

"Blessed is she who believed, for there will be a fulfillment of those things which were told her from the Lord."

Luke 1:45

Then Jesus answered and said to her, "O woman, great is your faith! Let it be to you as you desire." And her daughter was healed from that very hour.

Matthew 15:28

And they were both righteous before God, walking in all the commandments and ordinances of the Lord blameless.

Luke 1:6

Therefore, having been justified by faith, we have peace with God through our Lord Jesus Christ,

through whom also we have access by faith into this grace in which we stand, and rejoice in hope of the glory of God.

Romans 5:1–2

Family

❦

And they were both righteous before God, walking in all the commandments and ordinances of the Lord blameless.

Luke 1:6

And Eli would bless Elkanah and his wife, and say, "The LORD give you descendants from this woman for the loan that was given to the LORD." Then they would go to their own home.

I Samuel 2:20

He grants the barren woman a home,
Like a joyful mother of children.
Praise the LORD!

Psalm 113:9

But Ruth said:
"Entreat me not to leave you,
Or to turn back from following after you;
For wherever you go, I will go;
And wherever you lodge, I will lodge;
Your people shall be my people,
And your God, my God."

Ruth 1:16

"And when you go into a household, greet it.

"If the household is worthy, let your peace come upon it. But if it is not worthy, let your peace return to you."

Matthew 10:12–13

Favor

❧

Then God said: "No, Sarah your wife shall bear you a son, and you shall call his name Isaac; I will establish My covenant with him for an everlasting covenant, and with his descendants after him."

Genesis 17:19

"For he will be great in the sight of the Lord, and shall drink neither wine nor strong drink. He will also be filled with the Holy Spirit, even from his mother's womb.

"And he will turn many of the children of Israel to the Lord their God."

Luke 1:15–16

Then the angel said to her, "Do not be afraid, Mary, for you have found favor with God."

Luke 1:30

And the child Samuel grew in stature, and in favor both with the LORD and men.

I Samuel 2:26

Fulfillment

Then King David answered and said, "Call Bathsheba to me." So she came into the king's presence and stood before the king.

And the king took an oath and said, "As the LORD lives, who has redeemed my life from every distress,

"just as I swore to you by the LORD God of Israel, saying, 'Assuredly Solomon your son shall be king after me, and he shall sit on my throne in my place,' so I certainly will do this day."

I Kings 1:28–30

"And I will put enmity
Between you and the woman,
And between your seed and her Seed;
He shall bruise your head,
And you shall bruise His heel."

Genesis 3:15

Your wife shall be like a fruitful vine
In the very heart of your house,
Your children like olive plants
All around your table.

Psalm 128:3

Happiness
❧

And Sarah said, "God has made me laugh, and all who hear will laugh with me."

Genesis 21:6

Then Leah said, "I am happy, for the daughters will call me blessed." So she called his name Asher.

Genesis 30:13

"And you will have joy and gladness, and many will rejoice at his birth."

Luke 1:14

"And my spirit has rejoiced in God my Savior."

Luke 1:47

But let all those rejoice who put their trust in You;
Let them ever shout for joy, because You defend them;
Let those also who love Your name
Be joyful in You.
For You, O LORD, will bless the righteous;
With favor You will surround him as with a shield.

Psalm 5:11–12

Healing

❦

Now when Jesus had come into Peter's house, He saw his wife's mother lying sick with a fever.

So He touched her hand, and the fever left her. And she arose and served them.

Matthew 8:14–15

So Abraham prayed to God; and God healed Abimelech, his wife, and his female servants. Then they bore children.

Genesis 20:17

And suddenly, a woman who had a flow of blood for twelve years came from behind and touched the hem of His garment.

For she said to herself, "If only I may touch His garment, I shall be made well."

But Jesus turned around, and when He saw her He said, "Be of good cheer, daughter; your faith has made you well." And the woman was made well from that hour.

Matthew 9:20–22

Justice

❦

And the king said, "Divide the living child in two, and give half to one, and half to the other."

Then the woman whose son was living spoke to the king, for she yearned with compassion for her son; and she said, "O my lord, give her the living child, and by no means kill him!" But the other said, "Let him be neither mine nor yours, but divide him."

So the king answered and said, "Give the first woman the living child, and by no means kill him; she is his mother."

I Kings 3:25–27

Then Rachel said, "God has judged my case; and He has also heard my voice and given me a son." Therefore she called his name Dan.

Genesis 30:6

Marriage

Therefore a man shall leave his father and mother and be joined to his wife, and they shall become one flesh.

Genesis 2:24

Now Jacob loved Rachel; so he said, "I will serve you seven years for Rachel your younger daughter."

Genesis 29:18

And she said, "Let your maidservant find favor in your sight." So the woman went her way and ate, and her face was no longer sad.

I Samuel 1:18

Then Elkanah her husband said to her, "Hannah, why do you weep? Why do you not eat? And why is your heart grieved? Am I not better to you than ten sons?"

I Samuel 1:8

Her husband is known in the gates,
When he sits among the elders of the land.

Proverbs 31:23

Mercy

"Thus the Lord has dealt with me, in the days when He looked on me, to take away my reproach among people."

Luke 1:25

And the Angel of the LORD said to her:
"Behold, you are with child,
And you shall bear a son.
You shall call his name Ishmael,
Because the LORD has heard your affliction."

Genesis 16:11

Then God remembered Rachel, and God listened to her and opened her womb.

And she conceived and bore a son, and said, "God has taken away my reproach."

Genesis 30:22–23

And behold, a woman of Canaan came from that region and cried out to Him, saying, "Have mercy on me, O Lord, Son of David! My daughter is severely demon-possessed."

Then Jesus answered and said to her, "O woman, great is your faith! Let it be to you as you desire." And her daughter was healed from that very hour.

Matthew 15:22, 28

Miracles

❧

Then they said to him, "Where is Sarah your wife?" So he said, "Here, in the tent."

And He said, "I will certainly return to you according to the time of life, and behold, Sarah your wife shall have a son." (Sarah was listening in the tent door which was behind him.)

Now Abraham and Sarah were old, well advanced in age; and Sarah had passed the age of childbearing.

Therefore Sarah laughed within herself, saying, "After I have grown old, shall I have pleasure, my lord being old also?"

And the LORD said to Abraham, "Why did Sarah laugh, saying, 'Shall I surely bear a child, since I am old?'

"Is anything too hard for the LORD? At the appointed time I will return to you, according to the time of life, and Sarah shall have a son."

Genesis 18:9–14

She also said, "Who would have said to Abraham that Sarah would nurse children? For I have borne him a son in his old age."

Genesis 21:7

And His disciples asked Him, saying, "Rabbi, who sinned, this man or his parents, that he was born blind?"

Jesus answered, "Neither this man nor his parents sinned, but that the works of God should be revealed in him."

John 9:2–3

"Now indeed, Elizabeth your relative has also conceived a son in her old age; and this is now the sixth month for her who was called barren.

"For with God nothing will be impossible."

Luke 1:36–37

Then Jesus answered and said to her, "O woman, great is your faith! Let it be to you as you desire." And her daughter was healed from that very hour.

Matthew 15:28

Power

And it happened, when Elizabeth heard the greeting of Mary, that the babe leaped in her womb; and Elizabeth was filled with the Holy Spirit.

Luke 1:41

She girds herself with strength,
And strengthens her arms.

Proverbs 31:17

"But you shall receive power when the Holy Spirit has come upon you; and you shall be witnesses to Me in Jerusalem, and in all Judea and Samaria, and to the end of the earth."

Acts 1:8

Yet in all these things we are more than conquerors through Him who loved us.

Romans 8:37

Restoration

※

And may he be to you a restorer of life and a nourisher of your old age; for your daughter-in-law, who loves you, who is better to you than seven sons, has borne him."

Ruth 4:15

And Adam knew his wife again, and she bore a son and named him Seth, "For God has appointed another seed for me instead of Abel, whom Cain killed."

Genesis 4:25

Now after those days his wife Elizabeth conceived; and she hid herself five months, saying,

"Thus the Lord has dealt with me, in the days when He looked on me, to take away my reproach among people."

Luke 1:24–25

But God will redeem my soul from the power of the grave,
For He shall receive me.

Psalm 49:15

Truth

"However, when He, the Spirit of truth, has come, He will guide you into all truth; for He will not speak on His own authority, but whatever He hears He will speak; and He will tell you things to come."

John 16:13

I have no greater joy than to hear that my children walk in truth.

III John 1:4

"And you shall know the truth, and the truth shall make you free."

John 8:32

"Therefore if the Son makes you free, you shall be free indeed."

John 8:36

God's Answers
for Mothers

How to Trust in the Sufficiency of Jesus

And we have such trust through Christ toward God.
Not that we are sufficient of ourselves to think of anything as being from ourselves, but our sufficiency is from God.

II Corinthians 3:4–5

My help comes from the LORD,
Who made heaven and earth.
He will not allow your foot to be moved;
He who keeps you will not slumber.

Psalm 121:2–3

I can do all things through Christ who strengthens me.

Philippians 4:13

The LORD is my shepherd;
I shall not want.
He makes me to lie down in green pastures;
He leads me beside the still waters.
He restores my soul;
He leads me in the paths of righteousness
For His name's sake.

Yea, though I walk through the valley of the shadow
of death,
I will fear no evil;
For You are with me;
Your rod and Your staff, they comfort me.

Psalm 23:1–4

Seeing then that we have a great High Priest who
has passed through the heavens, Jesus the Son of God,
let us hold fast our confession.

For we do not have a High Priest who cannot sympathize with our weaknesses, but was in all points tempted
as we are, yet without sin.

Let us therefore come boldly to the throne of grace,
that we may obtain mercy and find grace to help in
time of need.

Hebrews 4:14–16

And He said to me, "My grace is sufficient for you,
for My strength is made perfect in weakness." Therefore
most gladly I will rather boast in my infirmities, that the
power of Christ may rest upon me.

II Corinthians 12:9

And when I saw Him, I fell at His feet as dead. But
He laid His right hand on me, saying to me, "Do not be
afraid; I am the First and the Last.

"I am He who lives, and was dead, and behold, I am alive forevermore. Amen. And I have the keys of Hades and of Death."

Revelation 1:17–18

How much more shall the blood of Christ, who through the eternal Spirit offered Himself without spot to God, cleanse your conscience from dead works to serve the living God?

Hebrews 9:14

"Now the blood shall be a sign for you on the houses where you are. And when I see the blood, I will pass over you; and the plague shall not be on you to destroy you when I strike the land of Egypt."

Exodus 12:13

But now in Christ Jesus you who once were far off have been brought near by the blood of Christ.

Ephesians 2:13

Jesus said to him, "I am the way, the truth, and the life. No one comes to the Father except through Me."

John 14:6

The LORD is your keeper;
The LORD is your shade at your right hand.

The LORD shall preserve you from all evil;
He shall preserve your soul.
The LORD shall preserve your going out and your
coming in
From this time forth, and even forevermore.

Psalm 121:5, 7–8

How to Grasp the Power of the Word

❧

Forever, O LORD,
Your word is settled in heaven.
Your faithfulness endures to all generations;
You established the earth, and it abides.

Psalm 119:89–90

For the word of God is living and powerful, and sharper than any two-edged sword, piercing even to the division of soul and spirit, and of joints and marrow, and is a discerner of the thoughts and intents of the heart.

Hebrews 4:12

The words of the LORD are pure words,
Like silver tried in a furnace of earth,
Purified seven times.
You shall keep them, O LORD,
You shall preserve them from this generation forever.

Psalm 12:6–7

And that from childhood you have known the Holy Scriptures, which are able to make you wise for salvation through faith which is in Christ Jesus.

All Scripture is given by inspiration of God, and is

profitable for doctrine, for reproof, for correction, for instruction in righteousness.

II Timothy 3:15–16

He sent His word and healed them,
And delivered them from their destructions.

Psalm 107:20

In the beginning was the Word, and the Word was with God, and the Word was God.

He was in the beginning with God.

All things were made through Him, and without Him nothing was made that was made.

In Him was life, and the life was the light of men.

John 1:1–4

"The grass withers, the flower fades,
But the word of our God stands forever."

Isaiah 40:8

"Heaven and earth will pass away, but My words will by no means pass away."

Luke 21:33

Hold fast the pattern of sound words which you have heard from me, in faith and love which are in Christ Jesus.

II Timothy 1:13

How to Hold on to Your Faith

❧

"Have I not commanded you? Be strong and of good courage; do not be afraid, nor be dismayed, for the LORD your God is with you wherever you go."

Joshua 1:9

We are hard-pressed on every side, yet not crushed; we are perplexed, but not in despair;

persecuted, but not forsaken; struck down, but not destroyed—

always carrying about in the body the dying of the Lord Jesus, that the life of Jesus also may be manifested in our body.

II Corinthians 4:8–10

But you, beloved, building yourselves up on your most holy faith, praying in the Holy Spirit,

keep yourselves in the love of God, looking for the mercy of our Lord Jesus Christ unto eternal life.

Jude 1:20–21

Beloved, while I was very diligent to write to you concerning our common salvation, I found it necessary to write to you exhorting you to contend earnestly for the faith which was once for all delivered to the saints.

Jude 1:3

"For with God nothing will be impossible."

Luke 1:37

And having shod your feet with the preparation of the gospel of peace;

above all, taking the shield of faith with which you will be able to quench all the fiery darts of the wicked one.

Ephesians 6:15–16

For we walk by faith, not by sight.

II Corinthians 5:7

"Behold, I am the LORD, the God of all flesh. Is there anything too hard for Me?"

Jeremiah 32:27

But recall the former days in which, after you were illuminated, you endured a great struggle with sufferings:

Therefore do not cast away your confidence, which has great reward.

But we are not of those who draw back to perdition, but of those who believe to the saving of the soul.

Hebrews 10:32, 35, 39

How to Overcome the Enemy

Put on the whole armor of God, that you may be able to stand against the wiles of the devil.

For we do not wrestle against flesh and blood, but against principalities, against powers, against the rulers of the darkness of this age, against spiritual hosts of wickedness in the heavenly places.

Therefore take up the whole armor of God, that you may be able to withstand in the evil day, and having done all, to stand.

Stand therefore, having girded your waist with truth, having put on the breastplate of righteousness.

Ephesians 6:11–14

Therefore submit to God. Resist the devil and he will flee from you.

Draw near to God and He will draw near to you. Cleanse your hands, you sinners; and purify your hearts, you double-minded.

James 4:7–8

The LORD shall preserve you from all evil;
He shall preserve your soul.

The LORD shall preserve your going out and your
coming in
From this time forth, and even forevermore.

Psalm 121:7–8

And the peace of God, which surpasses all understanding, will guard your hearts and minds through Christ
Jesus.

Finally, brethren, whatever things are true, whatever
things are noble, whatever things are just, whatever things
are pure, whatever things are lovely, whatever things are of
good report, if there is any virtue and if there is anything
praiseworthy—meditate on these things.

Philippians 4:7–8

"Be angry, and do not sin": do not let the sun go
down on your wrath,
nor give place to the devil.

Ephesians 4:26–27

But the Lord is faithful, who will establish you and
guard you from the evil one.

II Thessalonians 3:3

And the Lord will deliver me from every evil work
and preserve me for His heavenly kingdom. To Him be
glory forever and ever. Amen!

II Timothy 4:18

For in that He Himself has suffered, being tempted, He is able to aid those who are tempted.

Hebrews 2:18

"Beware of false prophets, who come to you in sheep's clothing, but inwardly they are ravenous wolves.

"You will know them by their fruits. Do men gather grapes from thornbushes or figs from thistles?

"Even so, every good tree bears good fruit, but a bad tree bears bad fruit."

"Therefore by their fruits you will know them.

"Not everyone who says to Me, 'Lord, Lord,' shall enter the kingdom of heaven, but he who does the will of My Father in heaven.

"Many will say to Me in that day, 'Lord, Lord, have we not prophesied in Your name, cast out demons in Your name, and done many wonders in Your name?'

"And then I will declare to them, 'I never knew you; depart from Me, you who practice lawlessness!'"

Matthew 7:15–17, 20–23

And do not be conformed to this world, but be transformed by the renewing of your mind, that you may prove what is that good and acceptable and perfect will of God.

Romans 12:2

And have no fellowship with the unfruitful works of darkness, but rather expose them.

Ephesians 5:11

Then the Lord knows how to deliver the godly out of temptations and to reserve the unjust under punishment for the day of judgment.

II Peter 2:9

Adulterers and adulteresses! Do you not know that friendship with the world is enmity with God? Whoever therefore wants to be a friend of the world makes himself an enemy of God.

James 4:4

Out of the same mouth proceed blessing and cursing. My brethren, these things ought not to be so.

Does a spring send forth fresh water and bitter from the same opening?

James 3:10–11

For the weapons of our warfare are not carnal but mighty in God for pulling down strongholds.

II Corinthians 10:4

How to Be Christ-Centered
❦

And now, little children, abide in Him, that when He appears, we may have confidence and not be ashamed before Him at His coming.

I John 2:28

Let the word of Christ dwell in you richly in all wisdom, teaching and admonishing one another in psalms and hymns and spiritual songs, singing with grace in your hearts to the Lord.

Colossians 3:16

Teaching us that, denying ungodliness and worldly lusts, we should live soberly, righteously, and godly in the present age,
　looking for the blessed hope and glorious appearing of our great God and Savior Jesus Christ.

Titus 2:12–13

But put on the Lord Jesus Christ, and make no provision for the flesh, to fulfill its lusts.

Romans 13:14

Looking unto Jesus, the author and finisher of our faith, who for the joy that was set before Him endured the cross, despising the shame, and has sat down at the right hand of the throne of God.

Hebrews 12:2

In You, O LORD, I put my trust;
Let me never be put to shame.
For You are my hope, O Lord GOD;
You are my trust from my youth.
Let my mouth be filled with Your praise
And with Your glory all the day.

Psalm 71:1, 5, 8

From the rising of the sun to its going down
The LORD'S name is to be praised.

Psalm 113:3

O God, You are my God;
Early will I seek You;
My soul thirsts for You;
My flesh longs for You
In a dry and thirsty land
Where there is no water.
So I have looked for You in the sanctuary,

To see Your power and Your glory.
My soul shall be satisfied as with marrow and fatness,
And my mouth shall praise You with joyful lips.
Because You have been my help,
Therefore in the shadow of Your wings I will rejoice.

Psalm 63:1–2, 5, 7

I will sing to the LORD as long as I live;
I will sing praise to my God while I have my being.
May my meditation be sweet to Him;
I will be glad in the LORD.

Psalm 104:33–34

"For in Him we live and move and have our being,
as also some of your own poets have said, 'For we are
also His offspring.'"

Acts 17:28

There is therefore now no condemnation to those
who are in Christ Jesus, who do not walk according to
the flesh, but according to the Spirit.

For the law of the Spirit of life in Christ Jesus has
made me free from the law of sin and death.

Romans 8:1–2

I sought the LORD, and He heard me,
And delivered me from all my fears.

Psalm 34:4

I have been crucified with Christ; it is no longer I who live, but Christ lives in me; and the life which I now live in the flesh I live by faith in the Son of God, who loved me and gave Himself for me.

Galatians 2:20

How to Have the Joy of the Lord

❧

"Come to Me, all you who labor and are heavy laden, and I will give you rest.

"Take My yoke upon you and learn from Me, for I am gentle and lowly in heart, and you will find rest for your souls.

"For My yoke is easy and My burden is light."

Matthew 11:28–30

But let all those rejoice who put their trust in You;
Let them ever shout for joy, because You defend them;
Let those also who love Your name
Be joyful in You.
For You, O LORD, will bless the righteous;
With favor You will surround him as with a shield.

Psalm 5:11–12

This is the day the LORD has made;
We will rejoice and be glad in it.

Psalm 118:24

Then he said to them, "Go your way, eat the fat, drink the sweet, and send portions to those for whom nothing is prepared; for this day is holy to our Lord. Do not sorrow, for the joy of the LORD is your strength."

Nehemiah 8:10

Let the saints be joyful in glory;
Let them sing aloud on their beds.

Psalm 149:5

A merry heart makes a cheerful countenance,
But by sorrow of the heart the spirit is broken.

Proverbs 15:13

"These things I have spoken to you, that My joy may remain in you, and that your joy may be full.

"This is My commandment, that you love one another as I have loved you."

John 15:11–12

My heart is steadfast, O God, my heart is steadfast;
I will sing and give praise.
Awake, my glory!
Awake, lute and harp!
I will awaken the dawn.
I will praise You, O Lord, among the peoples;
I will sing to You among the nations.

Psalm 57:7–9

Let your conduct be without covetousness; be content with such things as you have. For He Himself has said, "I will never leave you nor forsake you."

Hebrews 13:5

Because Your lovingkindness is better than life,
My lips shall praise You.
Thus I will bless You while I live;
I will lift up my hands in Your name.
My soul shall be satisfied as with marrow and fatness,
And my mouth shall praise You with joyful lips.

Psalm 63:3–5

For the kingdom of God is not eating and drinking,
but righteousness and peace and joy in the Holy Spirit.

Romans 14:17

Create in me a clean heart, O God,
And renew a steadfast spirit within me.
Do not cast me away from Your presence,
And do not take Your Holy Spirit from me.
Restore to me the joy of Your salvation,
And uphold me by Your generous Spirit.

Psalm 51:10–12

How to Face Trials

❧

The LORD is my shepherd;
I shall not want.
He makes me to lie down in green pastures;
He leads me beside the still waters.
He restores my soul;
He leads me in the paths of righteousness
For His name's sake.
Yea, though I walk through the valley of the shadow
of death, I will fear no evil;
For You are with me;
Your rod and Your staff, they comfort me.

Psalm 23:1–4

Do not rejoice over me, my enemy;
When I fall, I will arise;
When I sit in darkness,
The LORD will be a light to me.

Micah 7:8

I can do all things through Christ who strengthens me.

Philippians 4:13

And He said to me, "My grace is sufficient for you, for My strength is made perfect in weakness." Therefore most gladly I will rather boast in my infirmities, that the power of Christ may rest upon me.

II Corinthians 12:9

"When you pass through the waters, I will be
with you;
And through the rivers, they shall not overflow you.
When you walk through the fire, you shall not
be burned,
Nor shall the flame scorch you.
For I am the LORD your God,
The Holy One of Israel, your Savior;
I gave Egypt for your ransom,
Ethiopia and Seba in your place."

Isaiah 43:2–3

Deliver me out of the mire,
And let me not sink;
Let me be delivered from those who hate me,
And out of the deep waters.
Let not the floodwater overflow me,
Nor let the deep swallow me up;
And let not the pit shut its mouth on me.
Hear me, O LORD, for Your lovingkindness is good;

Turn to me according to the multitude of Your
tender mercies.
And do not hide Your face from Your servant,
For I am in trouble;
Hear me speedily.
Draw near to my soul, and redeem it;
Deliver me because of my enemies.

Psalm 69:14–18

The righteous cry out, and the LORD hears,
And delivers them out of all their troubles.
The LORD is near to those who have a broken heart,
And saves such as have a contrite spirit.
Many are the afflictions of the righteous,
But the LORD delivers him out of them all.

Psalm 34:17–19

Cast your burden on the LORD,
And He shall sustain you;
He shall never permit the righteous to be moved.

Psalm 55:22

In God I have put my trust;
I will not be afraid.
What can man do to me?
Vows made to You are binding upon me, O God;
I will render praises to You,

For You have delivered my soul from death.
Have You not kept my feet from falling,
That I may walk before God
In the light of the living?

Psalm 56:11–13

"But He knows the way that I take;
When He has tested me, I shall come forth as gold.
My foot has held fast to His steps;
I have kept His way and not turned aside."

Job 23:10–11

And I said, "This is my anguish;
But I will remember the years of the right hand of
the Most High."
I will remember the works of the LORD;
Surely I will remember Your wonders of old.
I will also meditate on all Your work,
And talk of Your deeds.
Your way, O God, is in the sanctuary;
Who is so great a God as our God?
You are the God who does wonders;
You have declared Your strength among the peoples.

Psalm 77:10–14

"Therefore do not worry, saying, 'What shall we
eat?' or 'What shall we drink?' or 'What shall we wear?'

"For after all these things the Gentiles seek. For your heavenly Father knows that you need all these things.

"But seek first the kingdom of God and His righteousness, and all these things shall be added to you.

"Therefore do not worry about tomorrow, for tomorrow will worry about its own things. Sufficient for the day is its own trouble."

Matthew 6:31–34

How to Overcome Stress

❧

"Therefore if the Son makes you free, you shall be free indeed."

John 8:36

Be anxious for nothing, but in everything by prayer and supplication, with thanksgiving, let your requests be made known to God;

and the peace of God, which surpasses all understanding, will guard your hearts and minds through Christ Jesus.

Finally, brethren, whatever things are true, whatever things are noble, whatever things are just, whatever things are pure, whatever things are lovely, whatever things are of good report, if there is any virtue and if there is anything praiseworthy—meditate on these things.

Philippians 4:6–8

"Peace I leave with you, My peace I give to you; not as the world gives do I give to you. Let not your heart be troubled, neither let it be afraid."

John 14:27

"Fear not, for I am with you;
Be not dismayed, for I am your God.
I will strengthen you,
Yes, I will help you,
I will uphold you with My righteous right hand."

Isaiah 41:10

But He was in the stern, asleep on a pillow. And they awoke Him and said to Him, "Teacher, do You not care that we are perishing?"

Then He arose and rebuked the wind, and said to the sea, "Peace, be still!" And the wind ceased and there was a great calm.

But He said to them, "Why are you so fearful? How is it that you have no faith?"

Mark 4:38–40

God is our refuge and strength,
A very present help in trouble.
Therefore we will not fear,
Even though the earth be removed,
And though the mountains be carried into the midst of the sea;
Though its waters roar and be troubled,
Though the mountains shake with its swelling.

Psalm 46:1–3

For God has not given us a spirit of fear, but of power and of love and of a sound mind.

Who has saved us and called us with a holy calling, not according to our works, but according to His own purpose and grace which was given to us in Christ Jesus before time began.

II Timothy 1:7, 9

"Come to Me, all you who labor and are heavy laden, and I will give you rest.

"Take My yoke upon you and learn from Me, for I am gentle and lowly in heart, and you will find rest for your souls.

"For My yoke is easy and My burden is light."

Matthew 11:28–30

How to Overcome Despair

I call to remembrance my song in the night;
I meditate within my heart,
And my spirit makes diligent search.

Psalm 77:6

But You, O LORD, are a shield for me,
My glory and the One who lifts up my head.
I cried to the LORD with my voice,
And He heard me from His holy hill.
I lay down and slept;
I awoke, for the LORD sustained me.
I will not be afraid of ten thousands of people
Who have set themselves against me all around.

Psalm 3:3–6

And He said to me, "My grace is sufficient for you, for My strength is made perfect in weakness." Therefore most gladly I will rather boast in my infirmities, that the power of Christ may rest upon me.

II Corinthians 12:9

Finally, brethren, whatever things are true, whatever things are noble, whatever things are just, whatever things are pure, whatever things are lovely, whatever things are of good report, if there is any virtue and if there is anything praiseworthy—meditate on these things.

Philippians 4:8

Through the LORD's mercies we are not consumed,
Because His compassions fail not.
They are new every morning;
Great is Your faithfulness.
"The LORD is my portion," says my soul,
"Therefore I hope in Him!"

Lamentations 3:22–24

Now may the God of hope fill you with all joy and peace in believing, that you may abound in hope by the power of the Holy Spirit.

Romans 15:13

I would have lost heart, unless I had believed
That I would see the goodness of the LORD
In the land of the living.
Wait on the LORD;
Be of good courage,
And He shall strengthen your heart;
Wait, I say, on the LORD!

Psalm 27:13–14

But those who wait on the LORD
Shall renew their strength;
They shall mount up with wings like eagles,
They shall run and not be weary,
They shall walk and not faint.

Isaiah 40:31

You are my hiding place and my shield;
I hope in Your word.

Psalm 119:114

What then shall we say to these things? If God is for us, who can be against us?

Romans 8:31

Yet in all these things we are more than conquerors through Him who loved us.

For I am persuaded that neither death nor life, nor angels nor principalities nor powers, nor things present nor things to come,

nor height nor depth, nor any other created thing, shall be able to separate us from the love of God which is in Christ Jesus our Lord.

Romans 8:37–39

How to Build a Life of Prayer

❧

"Again I say to you that if two of you agree on earth concerning anything that they ask, it will be done for them by My Father in heaven."

Matthew 18:19

As for me, I will call upon God,
And the LORD shall save me.
Evening and morning and at noon
I will pray, and cry aloud,
And He shall hear my voice.

Psalm 55:16–17

Be anxious for nothing, but in everything by prayer and supplication, with thanksgiving, let your requests be made known to God.

Philippians 4:6

Let us therefore come boldly to the throne of grace, that we may obtain mercy and find grace to help in time of need.

Hebrews 4:16

"Assuredly, I say to you, whatever you bind on earth will be bound in heaven, and whatever you loose on earth will be loosed in heaven."

Matthew 18:18

"And when you pray, you shall not be like the hypocrites. For they love to pray standing in the synagogues and on the corners of the streets, that they may be seen by men. Assuredly, I say to you, they have their reward.
"But you, when you pray, go into your room, and when you have shut your door, pray to your Father who is in the secret place; and your Father who sees in secret will reward you openly."

Matthew 6:5–6

Let us come before His presence with thanksgiving;
Let us shout joyfully to Him with psalms.

Psalm 95:2

"You will make your prayer to Him,
He will hear you,
And you will pay your vows.
You will also declare a thing,
And it will be established for you;
So light will shine on your ways."

Job 22:27–28

Likewise the Spirit also helps in our weaknesses. For we do not know what we should pray for as we ought, but the Spirit Himself makes intercession for us with groanings which cannot be uttered.

Romans 8:26

My voice You shall hear in the morning, O LORD;
In the morning I will direct it to You,
And I will look up.

Psalm 5:3

Now this is the confidence that we have in Him, that if we ask anything according to His will, He hears us.

And if we know that He hears us, whatever we ask, we know that we have the petitions that we have asked of Him.

I John 5:14–15

But without faith it is impossible to please Him, for he who comes to God must believe that He is, and that He is a rewarder of those who diligently seek Him.

Hebrews 11:6

How to Have God's Divine Protection

❧

"I am the good shepherd. The good shepherd gives
His life for the sheep."

John 10:11

Surely He shall deliver you from the snare of
the fowler
And from the perilous pestilence.
He shall cover you with His feathers,
And under His wings you shall take refuge;
His truth shall be your shield and buckler.
You shall not be afraid of the terror by night,
Nor of the arrow that flies by day,
Nor of the pestilence that walks in darkness,
Nor of the destruction that lays waste at noonday.
A thousand may fall at your side,
And ten thousand at your right hand;
But it shall not come near you.

Psalm 91:3–7

The angel of the LORD encamps all around those
who fear Him,
And delivers them.

Psalm 34:7

The LORD is my light and my salvation;
Whom shall I fear?
The LORD is the strength of my life;
Of whom shall I be afraid?
When the wicked came against me
To eat up my flesh,
My enemies and foes,
They stumbled and fell.
Though an army may encamp against me,
My heart shall not fear;
Though war may rise against me,
In this I will be confident.
One thing I have desired of the LORD,
That will I seek:
That I may dwell in the house of the LORD
All the days of my life,
To behold the beauty of the LORD,
And to inquire in His temple.
For in the time of trouble
He shall hide me in His pavilion;
In the secret place of His tabernacle
He shall hide me;
He shall set me high upon a rock.

Psalm 27:1–5

"When you pass through the waters, I will be with you;

And through the rivers, they shall not overflow you.
When you walk through the fire, you shall not
be burned,
Nor shall the flame scorch you."

Isaiah 43:2

"Are not two sparrows sold for a copper coin? And not one of them falls to the ground apart from your Father's will.

"But the very hairs of your head are all numbered.

"Do not fear therefore; you are of more value than many sparrows."

Matthew 10:29–31

So shall they fear
The name of the LORD from the west,
And His glory from the rising of the sun;
When the enemy comes in like a flood,
The Spirit of the LORD will lift up a standard
against him.

Isaiah 59:19

I will both lie down in peace, and sleep;
For You alone, O LORD, make me dwell in safety.

Psalm 4:8

"But whoever listens to me will dwell safely,
And will be secure, without fear of evil."

Proverbs 1:33

"For the mountains shall depart
And the hills be removed,
But My kindness shall not depart from you,
Nor shall My covenant of peace be removed,"
Says the LORD, who has mercy on you.
"All your children shall be taught by the LORD,
And great shall be the peace of your children.
No weapon formed against you shall prosper,
And every tongue which rises against you in judgment
You shall condemn.
This is the heritage of the servants of the LORD,
And their righteousness is from Me,"
Says the LORD.

Isaiah 54:10, 13, 17

The LORD is your keeper;
The LORD is your shade at your right hand.
The sun shall not strike you by day,
Nor the moon by night.
The LORD shall preserve you from all evil;
He shall preserve your soul.
The LORD shall preserve your going out and your
coming in
From this time forth, and even forevermore.

Psalm 121:5–8

How to Deal with Suffering
❧

Therefore, since Christ suffered for us in the flesh, arm yourselves also with the same mind, for he who has suffered in the flesh has ceased from sin,

that he no longer should live the rest of his time in the flesh for the lusts of men, but for the will of God.

I Peter 4:1–2

Beloved, do not think it strange concerning the fiery trial which is to try you, as though some strange thing happened to you;

but rejoice to the extent that you partake of Christ's sufferings, that when His glory is revealed, you may also be glad with exceeding joy.

If you are reproached for the name of Christ, blessed are you, for the Spirit of glory and of God rests upon you. On their part He is blasphemed, but on your part He is glorified.

But let none of you suffer as a murderer, a thief, an evildoer, or as a busybody in other people's matters.

Yet if anyone suffers as a Christian, let him not be ashamed, but let him glorify God in this matter.

For the time has come for judgment to begin at the

house of God; and if it begins with us first, what will be the end of those who do not obey the gospel of God?

I Peter 4:12–17

Now no chastening seems to be joyful for the present, but painful; nevertheless, afterward it yields the peaceable fruit of righteousness to those who have been trained by it.

Therefore strengthen the hands which hang down, and the feeble knees,

and make straight paths for your feet, so that what is lame may not be dislocated, but rather be healed.

Hebrews 12:11–13

We are hard-pressed on every side, yet not crushed; we are perplexed, but not in despair;

persecuted, but not forsaken; struck down, but not destroyed—

always carrying about in the body the dying of the Lord Jesus, that the life of Jesus also may be manifested in our body.

II Corinthians 4:8–10

For our light affliction, which is but for a moment, is working for us a far more exceeding and eternal weight of glory,

while we do not look at the things which are seen,

but at the things which are not seen. For the things which are seen are temporary, but the things which are not seen are eternal.

II Corinthians 4:17–18

But may the God of all grace, who called us to His eternal glory by Christ Jesus, after you have suffered a while, perfect, establish, strengthen, and settle you.

To Him be the glory and the dominion forever and ever. Amen.

I Peter 5:10–11

And if children, then heirs—heirs of God and joint heirs with Christ, if indeed we suffer with Him, that we may also be glorified together.

For I consider that the sufferings of this present time are not worthy to be compared with the glory which shall be revealed in us.

Romans 8:17–18

You therefore must endure hardship as a good soldier of Jesus Christ.

II Timothy 2:3

But we see Jesus, who was made a little lower than the angels, for the suffering of death crowned with glory and honor, that He, by the grace of God, might taste death for everyone.

Hebrews 2:9

For to this you were called, because Christ also suffered for us, leaving us an example, that you should follow His steps.

I Peter 2:21

For it was fitting for Him, for whom are all things and by whom are all things, in bringing many sons to glory, to make the captain of their salvation perfect through sufferings.

Hebrews 2:10

Though He was a Son, yet He learned obedience by the things which He suffered.

And having been perfected, He became the author of eternal salvation to all who obey Him.

Hebrews 5:8–9

I know how to be abased, and I know how to abound. Everywhere and in all things I have learned both to be full and to be hungry, both to abound and to suffer need.

I can do all things through Christ who strengthens me.

Philippians 4:12–13

This is a faithful saying:
For if we died with Him,
We shall also live with Him.

If we endure,
We shall also reign with Him.
If we deny Him,
He also will deny us.

II Timothy 2:11–12

Therefore let those who suffer according to the will of God commit their souls to Him in doing good, as to a faithful Creator.

I Peter 4:19

How to Obtain God's Promises
❧

By which have been given to us exceedingly great and precious promises, that through these you may be partakers of the divine nature, having escaped the corruption that is in the world through lust.

But also for this very reason, giving all diligence, add to your faith virtue, to virtue knowledge,

to knowledge self-control, to self-control perseverance, to perseverance godliness,

to godliness brotherly kindness, and to brotherly kindness love. For if these things are yours and abound, you will be neither barren nor unfruitful in the knowledge of our Lord Jesus Christ.

II Peter 1:4–8

Let us hold fast the confession of our hope without wavering, for He who promised is faithful.

Hebrews 10:23

Therefore do not cast away your confidence, which has great reward.

For you have need of endurance, so that after you have done the will of God, you may receive the promise:

"For yet a little while,
And He who is coming will
come and will not tarry."

Hebrews 10:35–37

"For assuredly, I say to you, whoever says to this mountain, 'Be removed and be cast into the sea,' and does not doubt in his heart, but believes that those things he says will be done, he will have whatever he says."

Mark 11:23

Now faith is the substance of things hoped for, the evidence of things not seen.

But without faith it is impossible to please Him, for he who comes to God must believe that He is, and that He is a rewarder of those who diligently seek Him.

By faith Sarah herself also received strength to conceive seed, and she bore a child when she was past the age, because she judged Him faithful who had promised.

Hebrews 11:1, 6, 11

"If you are willing and obedient,
You shall eat the good of the land;
But if you refuse and rebel,
You shall be devoured by the sword";
For the mouth of the LORD has spoken.

Isaiah 1:19–20

Now this is the confidence that we have in Him, that if we ask anything according to His will, He hears us.

And if we know that He hears us, whatever we ask, we know that we have the petitions that we have asked of Him.

I John 5:14–15

And said, "If you diligently heed the voice of the LORD your God and do what is right in His sight, give ear to His commandments and keep all His statutes, I will put none of the diseases on you which I have brought on the Egyptians. For I am the LORD who heals you."

Exodus 15:26

Behold, the LORD'S hand is not shortened,
That it cannot save;
Nor His ear heavy,
That it cannot hear.
But your iniquities have separated you from
your God;
And your sins have hidden His face from you,
So that He will not hear.

Isaiah 59:1–2

"But seek first the kingdom of God and His righteousness, and all these things shall be added to you."

Matthew 6:33

That you do not become sluggish, but imitate those who through faith and patience inherit the promises.

Hebrews 6:12

Scripture
Meditations for
Mothers

Meditations for Trust

❧

Those who trust in the LORD
Are like Mount Zion,
Which cannot be moved, but abides forever.
As the mountains surround Jerusalem,
So the LORD surrounds His people
From this time forth and forever.
For the scepter of wickedness shall not rest
On the land allotted to the righteous,
Lest the righteous reach out their hands to iniquity.
Do good, O LORD, to those who are good,
And to those who are upright in their hearts.
As for such as turn aside to their crooked ways,
The LORD shall lead them away
With the workers of iniquity.
Peace be upon Israel!

Psalm 125:1–5

When the LORD brought back the captivity of Zion,
We were like those who dream.
Then our mouth was filled with laughter,
And our tongue with singing.
Then they said among the nations,
"The LORD has done great things for them."

The LORD has done great things for us,
And we are glad.
Bring back our captivity, O LORD,
As the streams in the South.
Those who sow in tears
Shall reap in joy.
He who continually goes forth weeping,
Bearing seed for sowing,
Shall doubtless come again with rejoicing,
Bringing his sheaves with him.

Psalm 126:1–6

"Blessed are the poor in spirit,
For theirs is the kingdom of heaven.
Blessed are those who mourn,
For they shall be comforted.
Blessed are the meek,
For they shall inherit the earth.
Blessed are those who hunger and thirst for
righteousness,
For they shall be filled.
Blessed are the merciful,
For they shall obtain mercy.
Blessed are the pure in heart,
For they shall see God.
Blessed are the peacemakers,
For they shall be called sons of God.

Blessed are those who are persecuted for righteousness' sake,
For theirs is the kingdom of heaven.

Blessed are you when they revile and persecute you, and say all kinds of evil against you falsely for My sake.

Rejoice and be exceedingly glad, for great is your reward in heaven, for so they persecuted the prophets who were before you."

Matthew 5:3–12

LORD, how they have increased who trouble me!
Many are they who rise up against me.
Many are they who say of me,
"There is no help for him in God."
But You, O LORD, are a shield for me,
My glory and the One who lifts up my head.
I cried to the LORD with my voice,
And He heard me from His holy hill.
I lay down and slept;
I awoke, for the LORD sustained me.
I will not be afraid of ten thousands of people
Who have set themselves against me all around.
Arise, O LORD;
Save me, O my God!
For You have struck all my enemies on the cheekbone;

You have broken the teeth of the ungodly.
Salvation belongs to the LORD.
Your blessing is upon Your people.

Psalm 3:1–8

In the LORD I put my trust;
How can you say to my soul,
"Flee as a bird to your mountain"?
For look! The wicked bend their bow,
They make ready their arrow on the string,
That they may shoot secretly at the upright in heart.
If the foundations are destroyed,
What can the righteous do?
The LORD is in His holy temple,
The LORD's throne is in heaven;
His eyes behold,
His eyelids test the sons of men.
The LORD tests the righteous,
But the wicked and the one who loves violence His
soul hates.
Upon the wicked He will rain coals;
Fire and brimstone and a burning wind
Shall be the portion of their cup.
For the LORD is righteous,
He loves righteousness;
His countenance beholds the upright.

Psalm 11:1–7

For You will light my lamp;
The LORD my God will enlighten my darkness.
For by You I can run against a troop,
By my God I can leap over a wall.
As for God, His way is perfect;
The word of the LORD is proven;
He is a shield to all who trust in Him.
For who is God, except the LORD?
And who is a rock, except our God?
It is God who arms me with strength,
And makes my way perfect.
He makes my feet like the feet of deer,
And sets me on my high places.
He teaches my hands to make war,
So that my arms can bend a bow of bronze.
You have also given me the shield of Your salvation;
Your right hand has held me up,
Your gentleness has made me great.

Psalm 18:28–35

Meditations for Peace

✦

"All your children shall be taught by the LORD,
And great shall be the peace of your children.
In righteousness you shall be established;
You shall be far from oppression, for you shall
not fear;
And from terror, for it shall not come near you.
Indeed they shall surely assemble, but not because
of Me.
Whoever assembles against you shall fall for
your sake.
Behold, I have created the blacksmith
Who blows the coals in the fire,
Who brings forth an instrument for his work;
And I have created the spoiler to destroy.
No weapon formed against you shall prosper,
And every tongue which rises against you in
judgment
You shall condemn.
This is the heritage of the servants of the LORD,
And their righteousness is from Me,"
Says the LORD.

Isaiah 54:13–17

"The LORD will guide you continually,
And satisfy your soul in drought,
And strengthen your bones;
You shall be like a watered garden,
And like a spring of water, whose waters do
not fail."

Isaiah 58:11

"The Spirit of the Lord GOD is upon Me,
Because the LORD has anointed Me
To preach good tidings to the poor;
He has sent Me to heal the brokenhearted,
To proclaim liberty to the captives,
And the opening of the prison to those who are
bound;
To proclaim the acceptable year of the LORD,
And the day of vengeance of our God;
To comfort all who mourn,
To console those who mourn in Zion,
To give them beauty for ashes,
The oil of joy for mourning,
The garment of praise for the spirit of heaviness;
That they may be called trees of righteousness,
The planting of the LORD, that He may be
glorified."
And they shall rebuild the old ruins,
They shall raise up the former desolations,

And they shall repair the ruined cities,
The desolations of many generations.

Isaiah 61:1–4

The L ORD is my light and my salvation;
Whom shall I fear?
The L ORD is the strength of my life;
Of whom shall I be afraid?
When the wicked came against me
To eat up my flesh,
My enemies and foes,
They stumbled and fell.

Psalm 27:1–2

For in the time of trouble
He shall hide me in His pavilion;
In the secret place of His tabernacle
He shall hide me;
He shall set me high upon a rock.

Psalm 27:5

When my father and my mother forsake me,
Then the L ORD will take care of me.
I would have lost heart, unless I had believed
That I would see the goodness of the L ORD
In the land of the living.
Wait on the L ORD;

Be of good courage,
And He shall strengthen your heart;
Wait, I say, on the LORD!

Psalm 27:10, 13–14

The heavens declare the glory of God;
And the firmament shows His handiwork.

Psalm 19:1

Let the words of my mouth and the meditation of
my heart
Be acceptable in Your sight,
O LORD, my strength and my Redeemer.

Psalm 19:14

Meditations for Encouragement

❧

Out of the depths I have cried to You, O LORD;
Lord, hear my voice!
Let Your ears be attentive
To the voice of my supplications.
If You, LORD, should mark iniquities,
O Lord, who could stand?
But there is forgiveness with You,
That You may be feared.
I wait for the LORD, my soul waits,
And in His word I do hope.
My soul waits for the Lord
More than those who watch for the morning—
Yes, more than those who watch for the morning.
O Israel, hope in the LORD;
For with the LORD there is mercy,
And with Him is abundant redemption.
And He shall redeem Israel
From all his iniquities.

Psalm 130:1–8

I called on the LORD in distress;
The LORD answered me and set me in a broad place.
The LORD is on my side;

I will not fear.
What can man do to me?
The LORD is for me among those who help me;
Therefore I shall see my desire on those who hate me.
It is better to trust in the LORD
Than to put confidence in man.
It is better to trust in the LORD
Than to put confidence in princes.

Psalm 118:5–9

The LORD is my strength and song,
And He has become my salvation.
The voice of rejoicing and salvation
Is in the tents of the righteous;
The right hand of the LORD does valiantly.
The right hand of the LORD is exalted;
The right hand of the LORD does valiantly.
I shall not die, but live,
And declare the works of the LORD.

Psalm 118:14–17

"Do not remember the former things,
Nor consider the things of old.
Behold, I will do a new thing,
Now it shall spring forth;
Shall you not know it?

I will even make a road in the wilderness
And rivers in the desert."

Isaiah 43:18–19

Meditations of Praise

※

Oh, give thanks to the LORD, for He is good!
For His mercy endures forever.
Oh, give thanks to the God of gods!
For His mercy endures forever.
Oh, give thanks to the Lord of lords!
For His mercy endures forever:
To Him who alone does great wonders,
For His mercy endures forever;
To Him who by wisdom made the heavens,
For His mercy endures forever;
To Him who laid out the earth above the waters,
For His mercy endures forever;
To Him who made great lights,
For His mercy endures forever—
The sun to rule by day,
For His mercy endures forever;
The moon and stars to rule by night,
For His mercy endures forever.
To Him who struck Egypt in their firstborn,
For His mercy endures forever;
And brought out Israel from among them,
For His mercy endures forever;

With a strong hand, and with an outstretched arm,
For His mercy endures forever;
To Him who divided the Red Sea in two,
For His mercy endures forever;
And made Israel pass through the midst of it,
For His mercy endures forever;
But overthrew Pharaoh and his army in the Red Sea,
For His mercy endures forever;
To Him who led His people through the
wilderness,
For His mercy endures forever;
To Him who struck down great kings,
For His mercy endures forever;
And slew famous kings,
For His mercy endures forever—
Sihon king of the Amorites,
For His mercy endures forever;
And Og king of Bashan,
For His mercy endures forever—
And gave their land as a heritage,
For His mercy endures forever;
A heritage to Israel His servant,
For His mercy endures forever.
Who remembered us in our lowly state,
For His mercy endures forever;
And rescued us from our enemies,

For His mercy endures forever;
Who gives food to all flesh,
For His mercy endures forever.
Oh, give thanks to the God of heaven!
For His mercy endures forever.

Psalm 136:1–26

Because Your lovingkindness is better than life,
My lips shall praise You.
Thus I will bless You while I live;
I will lift up my hands in Your name.
My soul shall be satisfied as with marrow and fatness,
And my mouth shall praise You with joyful lips.
When I remember You on my bed,
I meditate on You in the night watches.
Because You have been my help,
Therefore in the shadow of Your wings I will rejoice.
My soul follows close behind You;
Your right hand upholds me.

Psalm 63:3–8

Let the saints be joyful in glory;
Let them sing aloud on their beds.
Let the high praises of God be in their mouth,
And a two-edged sword in their hand.

Psalm 149:5–6

Praise the LORD!
Praise God in His sanctuary;
Praise Him in His mighty firmament!
Praise Him for His mighty acts;
Praise Him according to His excellent greatness!
Praise Him with the sound of the trumpet;
Praise Him with the lute and harp!
Praise Him with the timbrel and dance;
Praise Him with stringed instruments and flutes!
Praise Him with loud cymbals;
Praise Him with clashing cymbals!
Let everything that has breath praise the LORD.
Praise the LORD!

Psalm 150:1–6

"I, Jesus, have sent My angel to testify to you these things in the churches. I am the Root and the Offspring of David, the Bright and Morning Star."

And the Spirit and the bride say, "Come!" And let him who hears say, "Come!" And let him who thirsts come. Whoever desires, let him take the water of life freely.

Revelation 22:16–17

My heart is steadfast, O God, my heart is steadfast;
I will sing and give praise.

Awake, my glory!
Awake, lute and harp!
I will awaken the dawn.
I will praise You, O Lord, among the peoples;
I will sing to You among the nations.

Psalm 57:7–9

Meditations on the Power of God

❦

"Where were you when I laid the foundations of
the earth?
Tell Me, if you have understanding.
Who determined its measurements?
Surely you know!
Or who stretched the line upon it?
To what were its foundations fastened?
Or who laid its cornerstone,
When the morning stars sang together,
And all the sons of God shouted for joy?
Or who shut in the sea with doors,
When it burst forth and issued from the womb;
When I made the clouds its garment,
And thick darkness its swaddling band;
When I fixed My limit for it,
And set bars and doors;
When I said,
'This far you may come, but no farther,
And here your proud waves must stop!'
Have you commanded the morning since your days
began,
And caused the dawn to know its place,

That it might take hold of the ends of the earth,
And the wicked be shaken out of it?
It takes on form like clay under a seal,
And stands out like a garment.
From the wicked their light is withheld,
And the upraised arm is broken.
Have you entered the springs of the sea?
Or have you walked in search of the depths?
Have the gates of death been revealed to you?
Or have you seen the doors of the shadow of death?
Have you comprehended the breadth of the earth?
Tell Me, if you know all this.
Where is the way to the dwelling of light?
And darkness, where is its place,
That you may take it to its territory,
That you may know the paths to its home?
Do you know it, because you were born then,
Or because the number of your days is great?
Have you entered the treasury of snow,
Or have you seen the treasury of hail,
Which I have reserved for the time of trouble,
For the day of battle and war?
By what way is light diffused,
Or the east wind scattered over the earth?
Who has divided a channel for the overflowing
water,
Or a path for the thunderbolt,

To cause it to rain on a land where there is no one,
A wilderness in which there is no man;
To satisfy the desolate waste,
And cause to spring forth the growth of tender grass?

Job 38:4–27

O LORD, our Lord,
How excellent is Your name in all the earth,
Who have set Your glory above the heavens!
Out of the mouth of babes and nursing infants
You have ordained strength,
Because of Your enemies,
That You may silence the enemy and the avenger.
When I consider Your heavens, the work of Your
fingers,
The moon and the stars, which You have ordained,
What is man that You are mindful of him,
And the son of man that You visit him?
For You have made him a little lower than the
angels,
And You have crowned him with glory and honor.
You have made him to have dominion over the
works of Your hands;
You have put all things under his feet,
All sheep and oxen—
Even the beasts of the field,
The birds of the air,

And the fish of the sea
That pass through the paths of the seas.
O LORD, our Lord,
How excellent is Your name in all the earth!

Psalm 8:1–9

At that time Jesus answered and said, "I thank You, Father, Lord of heaven and earth, that You have hidden these things from the wise and prudent and have revealed them to babes.

"Even so, Father, for so it seemed good in Your sight.

"All things have been delivered to Me by My Father, and no one knows the Son except the Father. Nor does anyone know the Father except the Son, and the one to whom the Son wills to reveal Him.

"Come to Me, all you who labor and are heavy laden, and I will give you rest.

"Take My yoke upon you and learn from Me, for I am gentle and lowly in heart, and you will find rest for your souls.

"For My yoke is easy and My burden is light."

Matthew 11:25–30

"I am He who lives, and was dead, and behold, I am alive forevermore. Amen. And I have the keys of Hades and of Death."

Revelation 1:18

"But hold fast what you have till I come.

"And he who overcomes, and keeps My works until the end, to him I will give power over the nations—

'He shall rule them with a rod of iron;
They shall be dashed to pieces like the potter's vessels'—
as I also have received from My Father;
and I will give him the morning star."

Revelation 2:25–28

"To him who overcomes I will grant to sit with Me on My throne, as I also overcame and sat down with My Father on His throne."

Revelation 3:21

Now I saw a new heaven and a new earth, for the first heaven and the first earth had passed away. Also there was no more sea.

Then I, John, saw the holy city, New Jerusalem, coming down out of heaven from God, prepared as a bride adorned for her husband.

And I heard a loud voice from heaven saying, "Behold, the tabernacle of God is with men, and He will dwell with them, and they shall be His people. God Himself will be with them and be their God.

"And God will wipe away every tear from their eyes; there shall be no more death, nor sorrow, nor crying. There shall be no more pain, for the former things have passed away."

Then He who sat on the throne said, "Behold, I make all things new." And He said to me, "Write, for these words are true and faithful."

And He said to me, "It is done! I am the Alpha and the Omega, the Beginning and the End. I will give of the fountain of the water of life freely to him who thirsts.

"He who overcomes shall inherit all things, and I will be his God and he shall be My son."

Revelation 21:1–7

I will love You, O LORD, my strength.
The LORD is my rock and my fortress and my deliverer;
My God, my strength, in whom I will trust;
My shield and the horn of my salvation, my stronghold.
I will call upon the LORD, who is worthy to be praised;
So shall I be saved from my enemies.
The pangs of death surrounded me,
And the floods of ungodliness made me afraid.
The sorrows of Sheol surrounded me;
The snares of death confronted me.
In my distress I called upon the LORD,
And cried out to my God;
He heard my voice from His temple,
And my cry came before Him, even to His ears.

Then the earth shook and trembled;
The foundations of the hills also quaked and were
shaken,
Because He was angry.
Smoke went up from His nostrils,
And devouring fire from His mouth;
Coals were kindled by it.
He bowed the heavens also, and came down
With darkness under His feet.
And He rode upon a cherub, and flew;
He flew upon the wings of the wind.
He made darkness His secret place;
His canopy around Him was dark waters
And thick clouds of the skies.
From the brightness before Him,
His thick clouds passed with hailstones and coals
of fire.
The LORD thundered from heaven,
And the Most High uttered His voice,
Hailstones and coals of fire.
He sent out His arrows and scattered the foe,
Lightnings in abundance, and He vanquished them.
Then the channels of the sea were seen,
The foundations of the world were uncovered
At Your rebuke, O LORD,
At the blast of the breath of Your nostrils.
He sent from above, He took me;

He drew me out of many waters.
He delivered me from my strong enemy,
From those who hated me,
For they were too strong for me.
They confronted me in the day of my calamity,
But the LORD was my support.
He also brought me out into a broad place;
He delivered me because He delighted in me.

Psalm 18:1–19

Meditations for Hope

❦

Through the LORD'S mercies we are not
consumed,
Because His compassions fail not.
They are new every morning;
Great is Your faithfulness.
"The LORD is my portion," says my soul,
"Therefore I hope in Him!"
The LORD is good to those who wait for Him,
To the soul who seeks Him.

Lamentations 3:22–25

I would have lost heart, unless I had believed
That I would see the goodness of the LORD
In the land of the living.
Wait on the LORD;
Be of good courage,
And He shall strengthen your heart;
Wait, I say, on the LORD!

Psalm 27:13–14

"Hear, O LORD, and have mercy on me;
LORD, be my helper!"
You have turned for me my mourning into dancing;

You have put off my sackcloth and clothed me with gladness.

Psalm 30:10–11

For He spoke, and it was done;
He commanded, and it stood fast.
The LORD brings the counsel of the nations to nothing;
He makes the plans of the peoples of no effect.

Psalm 33:9–10

We are hard-pressed on every side, yet not crushed; we are perplexed, but not in despair;

persecuted, but not forsaken; struck down, but not destroyed—

always carrying about in the body the dying of the Lord Jesus, that the life of Jesus also may be manifested in our body.

For we who live are always delivered to death for Jesus' sake, that the life of Jesus also may be manifested in our mortal flesh.

II Corinthians 4:8–11

For our light affliction, which is but for a moment, is working for us a far more exceeding and eternal weight of glory,

while we do not look at the things which are seen, but at the things which are not seen. For the things which are seen are temporary, but the things which are not seen are eternal.

II Corinthians 4:17–18

For we know that if our earthly house, this tent, is destroyed, we have a building from God, a house not made with hands, eternal in the heavens.

II Corinthians 5:1

What then shall we say to these things? If God is for us, who can be against us?

Romans 8:31

Who shall separate us from the love of Christ? Shall tribulation, or distress, or persecution, or famine, or naked-ness, or peril, or sword?

As it is written:

"For Your sake we are killed all day long;

We are accounted as sheep for the slaughter."

Yet in all these things we are more than conquerors through Him who loved us.

For I am persuaded that neither death nor life, nor angels nor principalities nor powers, nor things present nor things to come,

nor height nor depth, nor any other created thing, shall be able to separate us from the love of God which is in Christ Jesus our Lord.

Romans 8:35–39

"Ah, Lord GOD! Behold, You have made the heavens and the earth by Your great power and outstretched arm. There is nothing too hard for You.

"You show lovingkindness to thousands, and repay the iniquity of the fathers into the bosom of their children after them—the Great, the Mighty God, whose name is the LORD of hosts.

"You are great in counsel and mighty in work, for Your eyes are open to all the ways of the sons of men, to give everyone according to his ways and according to the fruit of his doings."

Jeremiah 32:17–19

But recall the former days in which, after you were illuminated, you endured a great struggle with sufferings:

partly while you were made a spectacle both by reproaches and tribulations, and partly while you became companions of those who were so treated.

Hebrews 10:32–33

Therefore do not cast away your confidence, which has great reward.

For you have need of endurance, so that after you have done the will of God, you may receive the promise:

"For yet a little while,
And He who is coming will come and will not tarry.

Now the just shall live by faith;
But if anyone draws back,
My soul has no pleasure in him."
But we are not of those who draw back to perdition,
but of those who believe to the saving of the soul.

Hebrews 10:35–39

Those who sow in tears
Shall reap in joy.
He who continually goes forth weeping,
Bearing seed for sowing,
Shall doubtless come again with rejoicing,
Bringing his sheaves with him.

Psalm 126:5–6

He heals the brokenhearted
And binds up their wounds.
He counts the number of the stars;
He calls them all by name.
Great is our Lord, and mighty in power;
His understanding is infinite.
The LORD lifts up the humble;
He casts the wicked down to the ground.
Sing to the LORD with thanksgiving;
Sing praises on the harp to our God,
Who covers the heavens with clouds,
Who prepares rain for the earth,

Who makes grass to grow on the mountains.
He gives to the beast its food,
And to the young ravens that cry.
He does not delight in the strength of the horse;
He takes no pleasure in the legs of a man.
The LORD takes pleasure in those who fear Him,
In those who hope in His mercy.

Psalm 147:3–11

For our light affliction, which is but for a moment, is working for us a far more exceeding and eternal weight of glory,

while we do not look at the things which are seen, but at the things which are not seen. For the things which are seen are temporary, but the things which are not seen are eternal.

II Corinthians 4:17–18

For we know that if our earthly house, this tent, is destroyed, we have a building from God, a house not made with hands, eternal in the heavens.

II Corinthians 5:1

"Come to Me, all you who labor and are heavy laden, and I will give you rest.

"Take My yoke upon you and learn from Me, for I

am gentle and lowly in heart, and you will find rest for your souls.

"For My yoke is easy and My burden is light."

Matthew 11:28–30

The LORD is my shepherd;
I shall not want.
He makes me to lie down in green pastures;
He leads me beside the still waters.
He restores my soul;
He leads me in the paths of righteousness
For His name's sake.
Yea, though I walk through the valley of the shadow of death,
I will fear no evil;
For You are with me;
Your rod and Your staff, they comfort me.
You prepare a table before me in the presence of my enemies;
You anoint my head with oil;
My cup runs over.
Surely goodness and mercy shall follow me
All the days of my life;
And I will dwell in the house of the LORD
Forever.

Psalm 23:1–6

Remember, O LORD, Your tender mercies and Your
lovingkindnesses,
For they are from of old.

Psalm 25:6

"You will keep him in perfect peace,
Whose mind is stayed on You,
Because he trusts in You.
Trust in the LORD forever,
For in YAH, the LORD, is everlasting strength.
For He brings down those who dwell on high,
The lofty city;
He lays it low,
He lays it low to the ground,
He brings it down to the dust.
The foot shall tread it down—
The feet of the poor
And the steps of the needy."
The way of the just is uprightness;
O Most Upright,
You weigh the path of the just.
Yes, in the way of Your judgments,
O LORD, we have waited for You;
The desire of our soul is for Your name
And for the remembrance of You.
With my soul I have desired You in the night,
Yes, by my spirit within me I will seek You early;

For when Your judgments are in the earth,
The inhabitants of the world will learn righteousness.

Isaiah 26:3–9

"To console those who mourn in Zion,
To give them beauty for ashes,
The oil of joy for mourning,
The garment of praise for the spirit of heaviness;
That they may be called trees of righteousness,
The planting of the LORD, that He may be glorified."
And they shall rebuild the old ruins,
They shall raise up the former desolations,
And they shall repair the ruined cities,
The desolations of many generations.
Strangers shall stand and feed your flocks,
And the sons of the foreigner
Shall be your plowmen and your vinedressers.
But you shall be named the priests of the LORD,
They shall call you the servants of our God.
You shall eat the riches of the Gentiles,
And in their glory you shall boast.

Isaiah 61:3–6

This hope we have as an anchor of the soul, both
sure and steadfast, and which enters the Presence behind
the veil.

Hebrews 6:19

And let us not grow weary while doing good, for in due season we shall reap if we do not lose heart.

Therefore, as we have opportunity, let us do good to all, especially to those who are of the household of faith.

Galatians 6:9–10

"Therefore do not worry about tomorrow, for tomorrow will worry about its own things. Sufficient for the day is its own trouble."

Matthew 6:34

Cast your burden on the LORD,
And He shall sustain you;
He shall never permit the righteous to be moved.

Psalm 55:22

Whenever I am afraid,
I will trust in You.
In God (I will praise His word),
In God I have put my trust;
I will not fear.
What can flesh do to me?

Psalm 56:3–4

In God I have put my trust;
I will not be afraid.
What can man do to me?

Vows made to You are binding upon me, O God;
I will render praises to You.

Psalm 56:11–12

But I will sing of Your power;
Yes, I will sing aloud of Your mercy in the morning;
For You have been my defense
And refuge in the day of my trouble.
To You, O my Strength, I will sing praises;
For God is my defense,
My God of mercy.

Psalm 59:16–17

Wait on the LORD,
And keep His way,
And He shall exalt you to inherit the land;
When the wicked are cut off, you shall see it.
I have seen the wicked in great power,
And spreading himself like a native green tree.
Yet he passed away, and behold, he was no more;
Indeed I sought him, but he could not be found.
Mark the blameless man, and observe the upright;
For the future of that man is peace.
But the transgressors shall be destroyed together;
The future of the wicked shall be cut off.
But the salvation of the righteous is from the LORD;
He is their strength in the time of trouble.

And the LORD shall help them and deliver them;
He shall deliver them from the wicked,
And save them,
Because they trust in Him.

Psalm 37:34–40

For in You, O LORD, I hope;
You will hear, O Lord my God.
For I said, "Hear me, lest they rejoice over me,
Lest, when my foot slips, they exalt themselves
against me."

Psalm 38:15–16

Therefore, in all things He had to be made like His
brethren, that He might be a merciful and faithful High
Priest in things pertaining to God, to make propitiation
for the sins of the people.

For in that He Himself has suffered, being tempted,
He is able to aid those who are tempted.

Hebrews 2:17–18

Then the Lord knows how to deliver the godly out
of temptations and to reserve the unjust under punishment for the day of judgment.

II Peter 2:9

For You, Lord, are good, and ready to forgive,
And abundant in mercy to all those who call
upon You.

Give ear, O LORD, to my prayer;
And attend to the voice of my supplications.
In the day of my trouble I will call upon You,
For You will answer me.
Among the gods there is none like You, O Lord;
Nor are there any works like Your works.

Psalm 86:5–8

But those who wait on the LORD
Shall renew their strength;
They shall mount up with wings like eagles,
They shall run and not be weary,
They shall walk and not faint.

Isaiah 40:31

The righteous shall flourish like a palm tree,
He shall grow like a cedar in Lebanon.
Those who are planted in the house of the LORD
Shall flourish in the courts of our God.
They shall still bear fruit in old age;
They shall be fresh and flourishing.

Psalm 92:12–14

Meditations for Faith

❦

Many are they who say of me,
"There is no help for him in God."
But You, O LORD, are a shield for me,
My glory and the One who lifts up my head.
I cried to the LORD with my voice,
And He heard me from His holy hill.
I lay down and slept;
I awoke, for the LORD sustained me.
I will not be afraid of ten thousands of people
Who have set themselves against me all around.
Arise, O LORD;
Save me, O my God!
For You have struck all my enemies on the
cheekbone;
You have broken the teeth of the ungodly.
Salvation belongs to the LORD.
Your blessing is upon Your people.

Psalm 3:2–8

But you, beloved, building yourselves up on your
most holy faith, praying in the Holy Spirit,

keep yourselves in the love of God, looking for the mercy of our Lord Jesus Christ unto eternal life.

Jude 1:20–21

"For with God nothing will be impossible."

Then Mary said, "Behold the maidservant of the Lord! Let it be to me according to your word." And the angel departed from her.

Now Mary arose in those days and went into the hill country with haste, to a city of Judah,

and entered the house of Zacharias and greeted Elizabeth.

And it happened, when Elizabeth heard the greeting of Mary, that the babe leaped in her womb; and Elizabeth was filled with the Holy Spirit.

Luke 1:37–41

Be anxious for nothing, but in everything by prayer and supplication, with thanksgiving, let your requests be made known to God;

and the peace of God, which surpasses all understanding, will guard your hearts and minds through Christ Jesus.

Philippians 4:6–7

Therefore, having been justified by faith, we have peace with God through our Lord Jesus Christ, through whom also we have access by faith into this grace in which we stand, and rejoice in hope of the glory of God.

And not only that, but we also glory in tribulations, knowing that tribulation produces perseverance;

and perseverance, character; and character, hope.

Now hope does not disappoint, because the love of God has been poured out in our hearts by the Holy Spirit who was given to us.

Romans 5:1–5

Now faith is the substance of things hoped for, the evidence of things not seen.

For by it the elders obtained a good testimony.

By faith we understand that the worlds were framed by the word of God, so that the things which are seen were not made of things which are visible.

By faith Abel offered to God a more excellent sacrifice than Cain, through which he obtained witness that he was righteous, God testifying of his gifts; and through it he being dead still speaks.

By faith Enoch was taken away so that he did not see death, "and was not found, because God had taken him"; for before he was taken he had this testimony, that he pleased God.

But without faith it is impossible to please Him,

for he who comes to God must believe that He is, and that He is a rewarder of those who diligently seek Him.

By faith Noah, being divinely warned of things not yet seen, moved with godly fear, prepared an ark for the saving of his household, by which he condemned the world and became heir of the righteousness which is according to faith.

By faith Abraham obeyed when he was called to go out to the place which he would receive as an inheritance. And he went out, not knowing where he was going.

By faith he dwelt in the land of promise as in a foreign country, dwelling in tents with Isaac and Jacob, the heirs with him of the same promise;

for he waited for the city which has foundations, whose builder and maker is God.

By faith Sarah herself also received strength to conceive seed, and she bore a child when she was past the age, because she judged Him faithful who had promised.

Therefore from one man, and him as good as dead, were born as many as the stars of the sky in multitude—innumerable as the sand which is by the seashore.

These all died in faith, not having received the promises, but having seen them afar off were assured of them, embraced them and confessed that they were strangers and pilgrims on the earth.

For those who say such things declare plainly that they seek a homeland.

And truly if they had called to mind that country from which they had come out, they would have had opportunity to return.

But now they desire a better, that is, a heavenly country. Therefore God is not ashamed to be called their God, for He has prepared a city for them.

By faith Abraham, when he was tested, offered up Isaac, and he who had received the promises offered up his only begotten son,

of whom it was said, "In Isaac your seed shall be called,"

concluding that God was able to raise him up, even from the dead, from which he also received him in a figurative sense.

By faith Isaac blessed Jacob and Esau concerning things to come.

By faith Jacob, when he was dying, blessed each of the sons of Joseph, and worshiped, leaning on the top of his staff.

By faith Joseph, when he was dying, made mention of the departure of the children of Israel, and gave instructions concerning his bones.

By faith Moses, when he was born, was hidden three months by his parents, because they saw he was a beautiful child; and they were not afraid of the king's command.

By faith Moses, when he became of age, refused to be called the son of Pharaoh's daughter,

choosing rather to suffer affliction with the people of God than to enjoy the passing pleasures of sin,

esteeming the reproach of Christ greater riches than the treasures in Egypt; for he looked to the reward.

By faith he forsook Egypt, not fearing the wrath of the king; for he endured as seeing Him who is invisible.

By faith he kept the Passover and the sprinkling of blood, lest he who destroyed the firstborn should touch them.

By faith they passed through the Red Sea as by dry land, whereas the Egyptians, attempting to do so, were drowned.

By faith the walls of Jericho fell down after they were encircled for seven days.

By faith the harlot Rahab did not perish with those who did not believe, when she had received the spies with peace.

And what more shall I say? For the time would fail me to tell of Gideon and Barak and Samson and Jephthah, also of David and Samuel and the prophets:

who through faith subdued kingdoms, worked righteousness, obtained promises, stopped the mouths of lions,

quenched the violence of fire, escaped the edge of the sword, out of weakness were made strong, became valiant in battle, turned to flight the armies of the aliens.

Women received their dead raised to life again.

Others were tortured, not accepting deliverance, that they might obtain a better resurrection.

Still others had trial of mockings and scourgings, yes, and of chains and imprisonment.

They were stoned, they were sawn in two, were tempted, were slain with the sword. They wandered about in sheepskins and goatskins, being destitute, afflicted, tormented—

of whom the world was not worthy. They wandered in deserts and mountains, in dens and caves of the earth.

And all these, having obtained a good testimony through faith, did not receive the promise,

God having provided something better for us, that they should not be made perfect apart from us.

Hebrews 11:1–40

Therefore we also, since we are surrounded by so great a cloud of witnesses, let us lay aside every weight, and the sin which so easily ensnares us, and let us run with endurance the race that is set before us,

looking unto Jesus, the author and finisher of our faith, who for the joy that was set before Him endured the cross, despising the shame, and has sat down at the right hand of the throne of God.

For consider Him who endured such hostility from sinners against Himself, lest you become weary and discouraged in your souls.

You have not yet resisted to bloodshed, striving against sin.

And you have forgotten the exhortation which speaks to you as to sons:

"My son, do not despise the chastening of the LORD,
Nor be discouraged when you are rebuked by Him;
For whom the LORD loves He chastens,
And scourges every son whom He receives."

If you endure chastening, God deals with you as with sons; for what son is there whom a father does not chasten?

But if you are without chastening, of which all have become partakers, then you are illegitimate and not sons.

Hebrews 12:1–8

For You will light my lamp;
The LORD my God will enlighten my darkness.
For by You I can run against a troop,
By my God I can leap over a wall.
As for God, His way is perfect;
The word of the LORD is proven;
He is a shield to all who trust in Him.
For who is God, except the LORD?
And who is a rock, except our God?

It is God who arms me with strength,
And makes my way perfect.
He makes my feet like the feet of deer,
And sets me on my high places.
He teaches my hands to make war,
So that my arms can bend a bow of bronze.
You have also given me the shield of Your salvation;
Your right hand has held me up,
Your gentleness has made me great.
You enlarged my path under me,
So my feet did not slip.
I have pursued my enemies and overtaken them;
Neither did I turn back again till they were destroyed.
I have wounded them,
So that they could not rise;
They have fallen under my feet.
For You have armed me with strength for the battle;
You have subdued under me those who rose up
against me.
You have also given me the necks of my enemies,
So that I destroyed those who hated me.
They cried out, but there was none to save;
Even to the LORD, but He did not answer them.

Psalm 18:28–41

God is our refuge and strength,
A very present help in trouble.

Therefore we will not fear,
Even though the earth be removed,
And though the mountains be carried into the
midst of the sea;
Though its waters roar and be troubled,
Though the mountains shake with its swelling.
There is a river whose streams shall make glad the
city of God,
The holy place of the tabernacle of the Most High.

Psalm 46:1–4

Whenever I am afraid,
I will trust in You.
In God (I will praise His word),
In God I have put my trust;
I will not fear.
What can flesh do to me?

Psalm 56:3–4

You number my wanderings;
Put my tears into Your bottle;
Are they not in Your book?
When I cry out to You,
Then my enemies will turn back;
This I know, because God is for me.
In God (I will praise His word),
In the LORD (I will praise His word),

In God I have put my trust;
I will not be afraid.
What can man do to me?

Psalm 56:8–11

My soul, wait silently for God alone,
For my expectation is from Him.
He only is my rock and my salvation;
He is my defense;
I shall not be moved.
In God is my salvation and my glory;
The rock of my strength,
And my refuge, is in God.
Trust in Him at all times, you people;
Pour out your heart before Him;
God is a refuge for us.

Psalm 62:5–8

Meditations for Victory

❧

I waited patiently for the LORD;
And He inclined to me,
And heard my cry.
He also brought me up out of a horrible pit,
Out of the miry clay,
And set my feet upon a rock,
And established my steps.
He has put a new song in my mouth—
Praise to our God;
Many will see it and fear,
And will trust in the LORD.
Blessed is that man who makes the LORD his trust,
And does not respect the proud, nor such as turn
aside to lies.
Many, O LORD my God, are Your wonderful works
Which You have done;
And Your thoughts toward us
Cannot be recounted to You in order;
If I would declare and speak of them,
They are more than can be numbered.
Sacrifice and offering You did not desire;
My ears You have opened.
Burnt offering and sin offering You did not require.

Then I said, "Behold, I come;
In the scroll of the book it is written of me.
I delight to do Your will, O my God,
And Your law is within my heart."
I have proclaimed the good news of righteousness
In the great assembly;
Indeed, I do not restrain my lips,
O LORD, You Yourself know.
I have not hidden Your righteousness within my
heart;
I have declared Your faithfulness and Your salvation;
I have not concealed Your lovingkindness and Your
truth
From the great assembly.
Do not withhold Your tender mercies from me,
O LORD;
Let Your lovingkindness and Your truth continually
preserve me.
For innumerable evils have surrounded me;
My iniquities have overtaken me, so that I am not
able to look up;
They are more than the hairs of my head;
Therefore my heart fails me.
Be pleased, O LORD, to deliver me;
O LORD, make haste to help me!
Let them be ashamed and brought to mutual
confusion

Who seek to destroy my life;
Let them be driven backward and brought to
dishonor
Who wish me evil.
Let them be confounded because of their shame,
Who say to me, "Aha, aha!"
Let all those who seek You rejoice and be glad in You;
Let such as love Your salvation say continually,
"The LORD be magnified!"
But I am poor and needy;
Yet the LORD thinks upon me.
You are my help and my deliverer;
Do not delay, O my God.

Psalm 40:1–17

Blessed is he who considers the poor;
The LORD will deliver him in time of trouble.
The LORD will preserve him and keep him alive,
And he will be blessed on the earth;
You will not deliver him to the will of his enemies.
The LORD will strengthen him on his bed of illness;
You will sustain him on his sickbed.

Psalm 41:1–3

The righteous cry out, and the LORD hears,
And delivers them out of all their troubles.
The LORD is near to those who have a broken heart,

And saves such as have a contrite spirit.
Many are the afflictions of the righteous,
But the LORD delivers him out of them all.

Psalm 34:17–19

Give us help from trouble,
For the help of man is useless.
Through God we will do valiantly,
For it is He who shall tread down our enemies.

Psalm 60:11–12

Speaking to one another in psalms and hymns and spiritual songs, singing and making melody in your heart to the Lord,

giving thanks always for all things to God the Father in the name of our Lord Jesus Christ.

Ephesians 5:19–20

"Have I not commanded you? Be strong and of good courage; do not be afraid, nor be dismayed, for the LORD your God is with you wherever you go."

Joshua 1:9

That the genuineness of your faith, being much more precious than gold that perishes, though it is tested by fire, may be found to praise, honor, and glory at the revelation of Jesus Christ,

whom having not seen you love. Though now you

do not see Him, yet believing, you rejoice with joy inexpressible and full of glory,

   receiving the end of your faith—the salvation of your souls.

I Peter 1:7–9

This is the day the LORD has made;
We will rejoice and be glad in it.
Save now, I pray, O LORD;
O LORD, I pray, send now prosperity.

Psalm 118:24–25

Then he said to them, "Go your way, eat the fat, drink the sweet, and send portions to those for whom nothing is prepared; for this day is holy to our Lord. Do not sorrow, for the joy of the LORD is your strength."

Nehemiah 8:10

He makes me to lie down in green pastures;
He leads me beside the still waters.
He restores my soul;
He leads me in the paths of righteousness
For His name's sake.
Yea, though I walk through the valley of the shadow of death,
I will fear no evil;
For You are with me;

Your rod and Your staff, they comfort me.
You prepare a table before me in the presence of
my enemies;
You anoint my head with oil;
My cup runs over.
Surely goodness and mercy shall follow me
All the days of my life;
And I will dwell in the house of the LORD
Forever.

Psalm 23:2–6

The earth is the LORD'S, and all its fullness,
The world and those who dwell therein.
For He has founded it upon the seas,
And established it upon the waters.
Who may ascend into the hill of the LORD?
Or who may stand in His holy place?
He who has clean hands and a pure heart,
Who has not lifted up his soul to an idol,
Nor sworn deceitfully.
He shall receive blessing from the LORD,
And righteousness from the God of his salvation.
This is Jacob, the generation of those who seek Him,
Who seek Your face.
Lift up your heads, O you gates!
And be lifted up, you everlasting doors!
And the King of glory shall come in.

Who is this King of glory?
The LORD strong and mighty,
The LORD mighty in battle.
Lift up your heads, O you gates!
Lift up, you everlasting doors!
And the King of glory shall come in.
Who is this King of glory?
The LORD of hosts,
He is the King of glory.

Psalm 24:1–10

To You, O LORD, I lift up my soul.
O my God, I trust in You;
Let me not be ashamed;
Let not my enemies triumph over me.

Psalm 25:1–2

The LORD shall preserve you from all evil;
He shall preserve your soul.
The LORD shall preserve your going out and your
coming in
From this time forth, and even forevermore.

Psalm 121:7–8

I was glad when they said to me,
"Let us go into the house of the LORD."

Psalm 122:1

The LORD is their strength,
And He is the saving refuge of His anointed.

Psalm 28:8

Commit your way to the LORD,
Trust also in Him,
And He shall bring it to pass.
He shall bring forth your righteousness as the light,
And your justice as the noonday.
Rest in the LORD, and wait patiently for Him;
Do not fret because of him who prospers in his way,
Because of the man who brings wicked schemes
to pass.
Cease from anger, and forsake wrath;
Do not fret—it only causes harm.
For evildoers shall be cut off;
But those who wait on the LORD,
They shall inherit the earth.

Psalm 37:5–9

The LORD is your keeper;
The LORD is your shade at your right hand.
The sun shall not strike you by day,
Nor the moon by night.
The LORD shall preserve you from all evil;
He shall preserve your soul.

The LORD shall preserve your going out and your coming in
From this time forth, and even forevermore.

Psalm 121:5–8

Oh, clap your hands, all you peoples!
Shout to God with the voice of triumph!
For the LORD Most High is awesome;
He is a great King over all the earth.
He will subdue the peoples under us,
And the nations under our feet.
He will choose our inheritance for us,
The excellence of Jacob whom He loves.
God has gone up with a shout,
The LORD with the sound of a trumpet.
Sing praises to God, sing praises!
Sing praises to our King, sing praises!
For God is the King of all the earth;
Sing praises with understanding.
God reigns over the nations;
God sits on His holy throne.
The princes of the people have gathered together,
The people of the God of Abraham.
For the shields of the earth belong to God;
He is greatly exalted.

Psalm 47:1–9

Great is the LORD, and greatly to be praised
In the city of our God,
In His holy mountain.

Psalm 48:1

I know how to be abased, and I know how to abound. Everywhere and in all things I have learned both to be full and to be hungry, both to abound and to suffer need.

I can do all things through Christ who strengthens me.

Nevertheless you have done well that you shared in my distress.

Philippians 4:12–14

Crisis Scripture Guide for Mothers

Addiction

Stand fast therefore in the liberty by which Christ has made us free, and do not be entangled again with a yoke of bondage.

Galatians 5:1

"And you shall know the truth, and the truth shall make you free."

John 8:32

Wine is a mocker,
Strong drink is a brawler,
And whoever is led astray by it is not wise.

Proverbs 20:1

Aging

❧

"For by me your days will be multiplied,
And years of life will be added to you."

Proverbs 9:11

Therefore remove sorrow from your heart,
And put away evil from your flesh,
For childhood and youth are vanity.

Ecclesiastes 11:10

The fear of the LORD prolongs days,
But the years of the wicked will be shortened.

Proverbs 10:27

Anger

Who, when He was reviled, did not revile in return; when He suffered, He did not threaten, but committed Himself to Him who judges righteously.

I Peter 2:23

"Be angry, and do not sin": do not let the sun go down on your wrath,
nor give place to the devil.

Ephesians 4:26–27

For God did not appoint us to wrath, but to obtain salvation through our Lord Jesus Christ.

I Thessalonians 5:9

Anxiety

❧

Peace I leave with you, My peace I give to you; not as the world gives do I give to you. Let not your heart be troubled, neither let it be afraid.

John 14:27

Let your gentleness be known to all men. The Lord is at hand.

Be anxious for nothing, but in everything by prayer and supplication, with thanksgiving, let your requests be made known to God;

and the peace of God, which surpasses all understanding, will guard your hearts and minds through Christ Jesus.

Finally, brethren, whatever things are true, whatever things are noble, whatever things are just, whatever things are pure, whatever things are lovely, whatever things are of good report, if there is any virtue and if there is anything praiseworthy—meditate on these things.

Philippians 4:5–8

God is our refuge and strength,
A very present help in trouble.
Therefore we will not fear,

Even though the earth be removed,
And though the mountains be carried into the
midst of the sea.

Psalm 46:1–2

Backsliding

❧

He who covers his sins will not prosper,
But whoever confesses and forsakes them will have
mercy.

Proverbs 28:13

Create in me a clean heart, O God,
And renew a steadfast spirit within me.
Do not cast me away from Your presence,
And do not take Your Holy Spirit from me.
Restore to me the joy of Your salvation,
And uphold me by Your generous Spirit.

Psalm 51:10–12

All that the Father gives Me will come to Me, and
the one who comes to Me I will by no means cast out.

John 6:37

Bereavement

❧

So when this corruptible has put on incorruption, and this mortal has put on immortality, then shall be brought to pass the saying that is written: "Death is swallowed up in victory."

"O Death, where is your sting?
O Hades, where is your victory?"

The sting of death is sin, and the strength of sin is the law.

But thanks be to God, who gives us the victory through our Lord Jesus Christ.

I Corinthians 15:54–57

He will swallow up death forever,
And the Lord GOD will wipe away tears from
all faces;
The rebuke of His people
He will take away from all the earth;
For the LORD has spoken.

Isaiah 25:8

But I do not want you to be ignorant, brethren, concerning those who have fallen asleep, lest you sorrow as others who have no hope.

For if we believe that Jesus died and rose again, even so God will bring with Him those who sleep in Jesus.

I Thessalonians 4:13–14

Bitterness

❧

Let all bitterness, wrath, anger, clamor, and evil speaking be put away from you, with all malice.

Ephesians 4:31

Looking carefully lest anyone fall short of the grace of God; lest any root of bitterness springing up cause trouble, and by this many become defiled.

Hebrews 12:15

But if you have bitter envy and self-seeking in your hearts, do not boast and lie against the truth.

This wisdom does not descend from above, but is earthly, sensual, demonic.

James 3:14–15

Carnality

❧

For where envy and self-seeking exist, confusion and every evil thing are there.

James 3:16

Knowing this, that our old man was crucified with Him, that the body of sin might be done away with, that we should no longer be slaves of sin.

For he who has died has been freed from sin.

Now if we died with Christ, we believe that we shall also live with Him,

knowing that Christ, having been raised from the dead, dies no more. Death no longer has dominion over Him.

Romans 6:6–9

That you put off, concerning your former conduct, the old man which grows corrupt according to the deceitful lusts,

and be renewed in the spirit of your mind,

and that you put on the new man which was created according to God, in true righteousness and holiness.

Ephesians 4:22–24

Condemnation

❧

There is therefore now no condemnation to those who are in Christ Jesus, who do not walk according to the flesh, but according to the Spirit.

Romans 8:1

"There is none who understands;
There is none who seeks after God.
They have all turned aside;
They have together become unprofitable;
There is none who does good, no, not one."

Romans 3:11–12

But we are all like an unclean thing,
And all our righteousnesses are like filthy rags;
We all fade as a leaf,
And our iniquities, like the wind,
Have taken us away.
And there is no one who calls on Your name,
Who stirs himself up to take hold of You;
For You have hidden Your face from us,
And have consumed us because of our iniquities.
But now, O LORD,

You are our Father;
We are the clay, and You our potter;
And all we are the work of Your hand.

Isaiah 64:6–8

Confusion

❧

"You will keep him in perfect peace,
Whose mind is stayed on You,
Because he trusts in You."

Isaiah 26:3

For God is not the author of confusion but of peace,
as in all the churches of the saints.

I Corinthians 14:33

"For My thoughts are not your thoughts,
Nor are your ways My ways," says the LORD.
"For as the heavens are higher than the earth,
So are My ways higher than your ways,
And My thoughts than your thoughts."

Isaiah 55:8–9

Death

❧

For none of us lives to himself, and no one dies to himself.

For if we live, we live to the Lord; and if we die, we die to the Lord. Therefore, whether we live or die, we are the Lord's.

Romans 14:7–8

"For I know that my Redeemer lives,
And He shall stand at last on the earth;
And after my skin is destroyed, this I know,
That in my flesh I shall see God,
Whom I shall see for myself,
And my eyes shall behold, and not another.
How my heart yearns within me!"

Job 19:25–27

He will swallow up death forever,
And the Lord GOD will wipe away tears from
all faces;
The rebuke of His people
He will take away from all the earth;
For the LORD has spoken.

Isaiah 25:8

Depression

Then he said to them, "Go your way, eat the fat, drink the sweet, and send portions to those for whom nothing is prepared; for this day is holy to our Lord. Do not sorrow, for the joy of the LORD is your strength."

Nehemiah 8:10

Finally, brethren, whatever things are true, whatever things are noble, whatever things are just, whatever things are pure, whatever things are lovely, whatever things are of good report, if there is any virtue and if there is anything praiseworthy—meditate on these things.

Philippians 4:8

And we know that all things work together for good to those who love God, to those who are the called according to His purpose.

Romans 8:28

Dissatisfaction

❦

Hell and Destruction are never full;
So the eyes of man are never satisfied.

Proverbs 27:20

Let your conduct be without covetousness; be content with such things as you have. For He Himself has said, "I will never leave you nor forsake you."
So we may boldly say:
"The LORD is my helper;
I will not fear.
What can man do to me?"

Hebrews 13:5–6

Now godliness with contentment is great gain.
For we brought nothing into this world, and it is certain we can carry nothing out.
And having food and clothing, with these we shall be content.

I Timothy 6:6–8

Doubt

❦

Draw near to God and He will draw near to you. Cleanse your hands, you sinners; and purify your hearts, you double-minded.

James 4:8

So then faith comes by hearing, and hearing by the word of God.

Romans 10:17

But recall the former days in which, after you were illuminated, you endured a great struggle with sufferings:

Therefore do not cast away your confidence, which has great reward.

For you have need of endurance, so that after you have done the will of God, you may receive the promise:

"For yet a little while,

And He who is coming will come and will not tarry.

Now the just shall live by faith;

But if anyone draws back,

My soul has no pleasure in him."

But we are not of those who draw back to perdition, but of those who believe to the saving of the soul.

Hebrews 10:32, 35–39

Failure

For a righteous man may fall seven times
And rise again,
But the wicked shall fall by calamity.
Do not rejoice when your enemy falls,
And do not let your heart be glad when he stumbles;
Lest the LORD see it, and it displease Him,
And He turn away His wrath from him.

Proverbs 24:16–18

The LORD upholds all who fall,
And raises up all who are bowed down.
The eyes of all look expectantly to You,
And You give them their food in due season.
You open Your hand
And satisfy the desire of every living thing.

Psalm 145:14–16

Not that we are sufficient of ourselves to think of anything as being from ourselves, but our sufficiency is from God.

II Corinthians 3:5

Fear

For God has not given us a spirit of fear, but of power and of love and of a sound mind.

II Timothy 1:7

I can do all things through Christ who strengthens me.

Philippians 4:13

And when I saw Him, I fell at His feet as dead. But He laid His right hand on me, saying to me, "Do not be afraid; I am the First and the Last.

"I am He who lives, and was dead, and behold, I am alive forevermore. Amen. And I have the keys of Hades and of Death."

Revelation 1:17–18

Finances

❧

"Therefore do not worry, saying, 'What shall we eat?' or 'What shall we drink?' or 'What shall we wear?'

"For after all these things the Gentiles seek. For your heavenly Father knows that you need all these things.

"But seek first the kingdom of God and His righteousness, and all these things shall be added to you.

"Therefore do not worry about tomorrow, for tomorrow will worry about its own things. Sufficient for the day is its own trouble."

Matthew 6:31–34

I have been young, and now am old;
Yet I have not seen the righteous forsaken,
Nor his descendants begging bread.
He is ever merciful, and lends;
And his descendants are blessed.

Psalm 37:25–26

And my God shall supply all your need according to His riches in glory by Christ Jesus.

Philippians 4:19

Illness

Is anyone among you sick? Let him call for the elders of the church, and let them pray over him, anointing him with oil in the name of the Lord.

James 5:14

He makes me to lie down in green pastures;
He leads me beside the still waters.
He restores my soul;
He leads me in the paths of righteousness
For His name's sake.
Yea, though I walk through the valley of the shadow of death,
I will fear no evil;
For You are with me;
Your rod and Your staff, they comfort me.

Psalm 23:2–4

Why are you cast down, O my soul?
And why are you disquieted within me?
Hope in God;
For I shall yet praise Him,
The help of my countenance and my God.

Psalm 43:5

Insecurity

❧

But the Lord is faithful, who will establish you and guard you from the evil one.

II Thessalonians 3:3

Surely He shall deliver you from the snare of
the fowler
And from the perilous pestilence.
He shall cover you with His feathers,
And under His wings you shall take refuge;
His truth shall be your shield and buckler.
You shall not be afraid of the terror by night,
Nor of the arrow that flies by day,
Nor of the pestilence that walks in darkness,
Nor of the destruction that lays waste at noonday.
A thousand may fall at your side,
And ten thousand at your right hand;
But it shall not come near you.

Psalm 91:3–7

And we have such trust through Christ toward God.
Not that we are sufficient of ourselves to think of anything as being from ourselves, but our sufficiency is from God.

II Corinthians 3:4–5

Judging

❧

Therefore judge nothing before the time, until the Lord comes, who will both bring to light the hidden things of darkness and reveal the counsels of the hearts. Then each one's praise will come from God.

I Corinthians 4:5

"And why do you look at the speck in your brother's eye, but do not consider the plank in your own eye?

"Hypocrite! First remove the plank from your own eye, and then you will see clearly to remove the speck from your brother's eye."

Matthew 7:3, 5

"For the Father judges no one, but has committed all judgment to the Son."

John 5:22

Loneliness

❧

"I will not leave you orphans; I will come to you."

John 14:18

He heals the brokenhearted
And binds up their wounds.

Psalm 147:3

When my father and my mother forsake me,
Then the LORD will take care of me.

Psalm 27:10

Lust

⁂

Then the Lord knows how to deliver the godly out of temptations and to reserve the unjust under punishment for the day of judgment.

II Peter 2:9

"If your hand or foot causes you to sin, cut it off and cast it from you. It is better for you to enter into life lame or maimed, rather than having two hands or two feet, to be cast into the everlasting fire.

"And if your eye causes you to sin, pluck it out and cast it from you. It is better for you to enter into life with one eye, rather than having two eyes, to be cast into hell fire."

Matthew 18:8–9

Do not lust after her beauty in your heart,
Nor let her allure you with her eyelids.
For by means of a harlot
A man is reduced to a crust of bread;
And an adulteress will prey upon his precious life.

Proverbs 6:25–26

Marriage

❧

Do not be unequally yoked together with unbelievers. For what fellowship has righteousness with lawlessness? And what communion has light with darkness?

And what accord has Christ with Belial? Or what part has a believer with an unbeliever?

And what agreement has the temple of God with idols? For you are the temple of the living God. As God has said:

"I will dwell in them
And walk among them.
I will be their God,
And they shall be My people."
Therefore
"Come out from among them
And be separate, says the Lord.
Do not touch what is unclean,
And I will receive you."

II Corinthians 6:14–17

Now to the married I command, yet not I but the Lord: A wife is not to depart from her husband.

But even if she does depart, let her remain unmarried

or be reconciled to her husband. And a husband is not to divorce his wife.

But to the rest I, not the Lord, say: If any brother has a wife who does not believe, and she is willing to live with him, let him not divorce her.

And a woman who has a husband who does not believe, if he is willing to live with her, let her not divorce him.

For the unbelieving husband is sanctified by the wife, and the unbelieving wife is sanctified by the husband; otherwise your children would be unclean, but now they are holy.

But if the unbeliever departs, let him depart; a brother or a sister is not under bondage in such cases. But God has called us to peace.

For how do you know, O wife, whether you will save your husband? Or how do you know, O husband, whether you will save your wife?

But as God has distributed to each one, as the Lord has called each one, so let him walk. And so I ordain in all the churches.

I Corinthians 7:10–17

Marriage is honorable among all, and the bed undefiled; but fornicators and adulterers God will judge.

Hebrews 13:4

Pride

Then Jesus called a little child to Him, set him in the midst of them,

and said, "Assuredly, I say to you, unless you are converted and become as little children, you will by no means enter the kingdom of heaven.

"Therefore whoever humbles himself as this little child is the greatest in the kingdom of heaven."

Matthew 18:2–4

Do not boast about tomorrow,
For you do not know what a day may bring forth.
Let another man praise you, and not your own mouth;
A stranger, and not your own lips.

Proverbs 27:1–2

"The Pharisee stood and prayed thus with himself, 'God, I thank You that I am not like other men—extortioners, unjust, adulterers, or even as this tax collector.

'I fast twice a week; I give tithes of all that I possess.'

"And the tax collector, standing afar off, would not so much as raise his eyes to heaven, but beat his breast, saying, 'God, be merciful to me a sinner!'

"I tell you, this man went down to his house justified

rather than the other; for everyone who exalts himself will be humbled, and he who humbles himself will be exalted."

Luke 18:11–14

Satan

❖

Finally, my brethren, be strong in the Lord and in the power of His might.

Put on the whole armor of God, that you may be able to stand against the wiles of the devil.

For we do not wrestle against flesh and blood, but against principalities, against powers, against the rulers of the darkness of this age, against spiritual hosts of wickedness in the heavenly places.

Therefore take up the whole armor of God, that you may be able to withstand in the evil day, and having done all, to stand.

Stand therefore, having girded your waist with truth, having put on the breastplate of righteousness,

and having shod your feet with the preparation of the gospel of peace;

above all, taking the shield of faith with which you will be able to quench all the fiery darts of the wicked one.

And take the helmet of salvation, and the sword of the Spirit, which is the word of God.

Ephesians 6:10–17

Beloved, do not believe every spirit, but test the spirits, whether they are of God; because many false prophets have gone out into the world.

By this you know the Spirit of God: Every spirit that confesses that Jesus Christ has come in the flesh is of God,

and every spirit that does not confess that Jesus Christ has come in the flesh is not of God. And this is the spirit of the Antichrist, which you have heard was coming, and is now already in the world.

I John 4:1–3

And He said to them, "I saw Satan fall like lightning from heaven.

"Behold, I give you the authority to trample on serpents and scorpions, and over all the power of the enemy, and nothing shall by any means hurt you."

Luke 10:18–19

Suffering

Though He was a Son, yet He learned obedience by the things which He suffered.

And having been perfected, He became the author of eternal salvation to all who obey Him.

Hebrews 5:8–9

We are hard-pressed on every side, yet not crushed; we are perplexed, but not in despair;

persecuted, but not forsaken; struck down, but not destroyed—

always carrying about in the body the dying of the Lord Jesus, that the life of Jesus also may be manifested in our body.

II Corinthians 4:8–10

Therefore let those who suffer according to the will of God commit their souls to Him in doing good, as to a faithful Creator.

I Peter 4:19

Temptation

Blessed is the man who endures temptation; for when he has been approved, he will receive the crown of life which the Lord has promised to those who love Him.

James 1:12

Then the Lord knows how to deliver the godly out of temptations and to reserve the unjust under punishment for the day of judgment.

II Peter 2:9

My brethren, count it all joy when you fall into various trials,
knowing that the testing of your faith produces patience.
But let patience have its perfect work, that you may be perfect and complete, lacking nothing.

James 1:2–4

Trials

You therefore must endure hardship as a good soldier of Jesus Christ.

II Timothy 2:3

Beloved, do not think it strange concerning the fiery trial which is to try you, as though some strange thing happened to you;

but rejoice to the extent that you partake of Christ's sufferings, that when His glory is revealed, you may also be glad with exceeding joy.

I Peter 4:12–13

The righteous cry out, and the LORD hears,
And delivers them out of all their troubles.

Psalm 34:17

Weakness

⚜

And He said to me, "My grace is sufficient for you, for My strength is made perfect in weakness." Therefore most gladly I will rather boast in my infirmities, that the power of Christ may rest upon me.

II Corinthians 12:9

"Come to Me, all you who labor and are heavy laden, and I will give you rest.

"Take My yoke upon you and learn from Me, for I am gentle and lowly in heart, and you will find rest for your souls.

"For My yoke is easy and My burden is light."

Matthew 11:28–30

My help comes from the LORD,
Who made heaven and earth.
He will not allow your foot to be moved;
He who keeps you will not slumber.

Psalm 121:2–3

Worldliness

❧

"Now these are the ones sown among thorns; they are the ones who hear the word,

"and the cares of this world, the deceitfulness of riches, and the desires for other things entering in choke the word, and it becomes unfruitful.

"But these are the ones sown on good ground, those who hear the word, accept it, and bear fruit: some thirtyfold, some sixty, and some a hundred."

Mark 4:18–20

Who is he who overcomes the world, but he who believes that Jesus is the Son of God?

I John 5:5

Do not love the world or the things in the world. If anyone loves the world, the love of the Father is not in him.

For all that is in the world—the lust of the flesh, the lust of the eyes, and the pride of life—is not of the Father but is of the world.

And the world is passing away, and the lust of it; but he who does the will of God abides forever.

I John 2:15–17

SPECIAL BIRTHDAYS

My Children _____

_____

_____

_____

_____

_____

_____

_____

_____

_____

_____

_____

_____

_____

_____

_____

_____

_____

_____

_____

_____

_____

SPECIAL BIRTHDAYS

My Grandchildren _____

_____

_____

_____

_____

_____

_____

_____

_____

_____

_____

_____

_____

_____

_____

_____

_____

_____

_____

SPECIAL BIRTHDAYS

Other _____

_____

_____

_____

_____

_____

_____

_____

_____

_____

_____

_____

_____

_____

_____

_____

_____

_____

_____

_____

_____

_____

MOTHER'S PRAYER NOTES

_____

_____

_____

_____

_____

_____

_____

_____

_____

_____

_____

_____

_____

_____

_____

_____

_____

_____

_____

_____

MOTHER'S PRAYER NOTES

_____

_____

_____

_____

_____

_____

_____

_____

_____

_____

_____

_____

_____

_____

_____

_____

_____

_____

_____

_____

_____

_____

MOTHER'S PRAYER NOTES

MOTHER'S PRAYER NOTES

_____
_____
_____
_____
_____
_____
_____
_____
_____
_____
_____
_____
_____
_____
_____
_____
_____
_____
_____
_____
_____
_____

MOTHER'S PRAYER NOTES

MOTHER'S PRAYER NOTES

_____
_____
_____
_____
_____
_____
_____
_____
_____
_____
_____
_____
_____
_____
_____
_____
_____
_____
_____
_____
_____
_____

MOTHER'S PRAYER NOTES

_____
_____
_____
_____
_____
_____
_____
_____
_____
_____
_____
_____
_____
_____
_____
_____
_____
_____
_____
_____

MOTHER'S PRAYER NOTES

_____
_____
_____
_____
_____
_____
_____
_____
_____
_____
_____
_____
_____
_____
_____
_____
_____
_____
_____
_____
_____
_____

MOTHER'S PRAYER NOTES

_____

_____

_____

_____

_____

_____

_____

_____

_____

_____

_____

_____

_____

_____

_____

_____

_____

_____

_____

_____

_____

_____

MOTHER'S PRAYER NOTES

_____
_____
_____
_____
_____
_____
_____
_____
_____
_____
_____
_____
_____
_____
_____
_____
_____
_____
_____
_____
_____
_____
_____

MOTHER'S PRAYER NOTES

MOTHER'S PRAYER NOTES

_____
_____
_____
_____
_____
_____
_____
_____
_____
_____
_____
_____
_____
_____
_____
_____
_____
_____
_____
_____
_____
_____